Christian

Child

Development

By Iris V. Cully

Change, Conflict, and Self-Determination
Children in the Church
Christian Child Development
Christian Worship and Church Education
The Dynamics of Christian Education
Imparting the Word: The Bible in Christian Education
New Life for Your Sunday School
Ways to Teach Children

With Kendig Brubaker Cully

From Aaron to Zerubbabel: Profiles of Bible People
An Introductory Theological Wordbook
Two Seasons: Advent and Lent

Christian

Child

Development

IRIS V. CULLY

Published in San Francisco by Harper & Row, Publishers

NEW YORK HAGERSTOWN SAN FRANCISCO LONDON

To the people
at Lexington Theological Seminary

Designed by Jim Mennick

Library of Congress Cataloging in Publication Data

Cully, Iris V.
CHRISTIAN CHILD DEVELOPMENT

Includes index.
1. Christian education of children. 2. Children—
Religious life. 3. Child Development. I. Title.
BV1475.2.C814 1979   268'.432   78–19507
ISBN 0–06–061648–2

79 80 81 82 83   10 9 8 7 6 5 4 3 2

Contents

Preface   *vii*

1   The Child Grows   *1*
2   The Child Thinks   *16*
3   The Child Feels   *33*
4   Aspects of Learning   *48*
5   Religious Development   *62*
6   Growing into Moral Persons   *75*
7   A Child's Commitment   *88*
8   Religious Development and the Family   *104*
9   The Child in the Christian Community   *116*
10 Ways of Teaching   *128*
11 The Bible Speaks to Children   *143*

Notes   *157*

Index   *163*

Preface

T H E responsibility for teaching the faith to children, long ago laid upon parents and the religious community, is always affected by basic understandings of learning held within a culture. Origen and Augustine, in their times, were aware of current teaching methods. During the twentieth century, especially since the founding of The Religious Education Association of the United States and Canada in 1903, teachers of religion have been especially attuned to insights from general education.

For this reason it is important now to ask how the religious education and development of children can be enriched by thinking and research from contemporary psychologists and educators such as Erik H. Erikson, B.F. Skinner, Jean Piaget, and Jerome Bruner. Several writers have expanded their perspective to include religious development: Ronald Goldman, working with cognitive learning, Marc Oraison, André Godin, and others associated with the Lumen Vitae Institute, using psychoanalytic insights.

This book applies such findings specifically to the religious education of children from birth to the age of twelve. It is addressed to teachers, parents, and, I hope, both Catholic and Protestant pastors, as well as to professors and students in colleges and seminaries providing professional preparation for ministry. Teachers and parents have an immediate and practical need; those in professional schools need both theory and practice; and clergy certainly will look for help in understanding the youngest members of the parish.

The first chapter traces the developmental stages as outlined by Erikson and draws implications for religious education in the church. Succeeding chapters take into account the work of Piaget, the critique of a cognitive approach by Richard M. Jones, and the implications of Skinner's theory of conditioned learning. The book next turns to an overview of religious development, including moral development and the meaning of commitment, followed by a consideration of the roles of family and church. Concluding chapters take up underlying methodology, practical teaching methods, and approaches to teaching the Bible in particular.

The need for religious education is usually taken for granted. Frequently it centers in the education of children and often is expressed primarily through the Sunday school or Confraternity of Christian Doctrine classes. But if we say there is a need, we must also be able to define the goals of religious education, and when we attempt to do this, little consensus may be found. Some people will say, "We want children to learn the content of the Bible." Usually this desire implies that the content be understood in historical or contemporary contexts. They want the Bible to apply to life (see Chapter 11). Others feel that the goal is commitment to

Christ. (Understandings of this goal are discussed in Chapter 7.) In some denominations the structure of belief is important. Since early times an understanding of the Apostles' Creed, the baptismal statement, has been an important element for instruction. Other people, realizing that no one is a Christian alone, insist that loyalty to and incorporation into the life of the church are essential. Most people would say that Christianity, however interpreted, is a way of life, and that the goal of Christian education has not been met unless there is some ability to reflect on one's actions in Christian terms and make decisions accordingly at whatever personal cost.

Because many people are involved in religious education —parents, teachers, pastors, and even the whole congregation—there will be differences in the importance attached to any or all of these goals. We need to think about these differences while reading about ways contemporary educational insights can be helpful to the task. We must remember also that religious education goals should be specific; there should be some way of recognizing that they have been accomplished. These should be goals that are not being met by another institution, because they pertain to life as a Christian. The trend in church education today is to encourage each parish to consider its own goals and choose curricular materials and teaching experiences most suited to effecting these goals. This is the reason, for instance, that three different planning guides were written for *Christian Education: Shared Approaches,* a church school curriculum developed recently by several Protestant denominations working together.

Quotations from the Bible in this book are from The Revised Standard Version unless otherwise noted.

It has been a number of years since my earlier book, *Children in the Church* (Philadelphia: Westminster Press, 1960) was a Pastoral Psychology Book Club selection and an alternate selection of the Religious Book Club. The book was used widely by religious education teachers, as well as by parents and pastors, and the appreciation they have expressed encouraged my resolve to do another book that would embody further insights into how children can and do learn about the Christian faith and how they can be guided in their development in faith. This book is the fulfillment of that resolve.

Once again I record thanks to my husband, Kendig, in this, my eighth book (in addition to the three we have written together). He encourages writing, patiently edits, and persistently urges until the completed manuscript is on its way to production. With deepest gratitude to God I affirm the joy of this symbiotic relationship, surely the most wonderful gift granted human beings.

Iris V. Cully

Lexington Theological Seminary
Lexington, Kentucky

CHAPTER 1

The Child

Grows

T H E persistent growth of creatures is one of life's won-
ders. Human parents watch this progression with joy, and
sometimes with misgiving. It is the privilege of an economically developed culture. Until late in the nineteenth century
in Europe (and in other parts of the world even today), only
50 percent of the infants born would live long enough for
their development to be noted. Often there was merely a
brief childhood for those who survived. Comforted by the
near presence of mothers, they shared in the basic tasks of
existence, tended younger children, and took their places
early at work in field or factory. One saw them tending vege-

tables in the United States or working at rug looms in Iran or India.

Like all else living on earth, children are born with the natural expectation of growing to maturity. Neither the promise of the Christian gospel nor the ideals of a society are fulfilled while many die young or waste away during adolescence.

Some years ago, the psychologist Robert Havighurst pointed out the cultural skills that children need to develop in order to live fully.[1] They must be able to talk in order to communicate with other people; to walk in order to move beyond the family and broaden their experiences; to distinguish right from wrong as established by the community. Physical skills learned during middle childhood facilitate participation in group games, while skills for reading, writing, and calculating bring achievement in school. Development of positive attitudes toward the self and others and the ability to get along with others fosters human interaction. These are developmental tasks. Each arises at a specific point, and the completion leads to success with later tasks. Conversely, when a task is not accomplished (talking, walking) there will be difficulty with later tasks as well as discomfort with the self and less ability to relate to others.

Erik Erikson, a well-known and widely read psychologist with psychoanalytic background, has outlined developmental tasks with less emphasis on cultural concerns and more attention to the effects on emotional development.[2] From studies of children he developed his own way of describing how they grow, using words that have theological as well as psychological significance: *trust, faith, identity.* These words are easily translated into religious categories. They give to us who are concerned with the development of faith handles by which to assess the religious significance of each stage and to become aware of ways by which we can understand our task in religious education with reference to the needs of children at each stage.

Erikson defines developmental tasks as "psycho-social crises precipitated both by the individual's readiness and by society's pressures." Each person goes through a series of life stages: a time when a capacity first appears or a period when it is so well-established and integrated that the next stage can be safely initiated. At the "end" of a stage, a psycho-social crisis appears (to use Erikson's term), and the person makes an unconscious decision either to go forward or to remain in the same stage. Lest this seem to be a ladder of accomplishment, or a series of stairs whereon one pauses briefly at each stage, it should be emphasized that development is not this orderly. Each stage is carried into the next stage. One says to a child who suddenly bursts into angry tears, "Don't act like a baby!" Even adults continue to seek occasionally the comforting assurances of infancy. Only when a person characteristically acts younger is such behavior noticeable. Erikson develops these stages through adulthood, but for our purposes it is sufficient to do so through the age of eleven.

The Infant (About the First Year): Basic Trust vs. Basic Mistrust

With this background, consider the growing child. The newborn infant is helpless, deprived of the automatically nurturing environment of prenatal days. The atmosphere is strange, food comes at uncertain times, covering is abrasive, different hands touch in new ways. Out of this situation will be learned trust or mistrust—of the self, others, and the situation. It all depends on the *quality* of the relationships with whoever is nurturing the child. This first stage (sometimes referred to as the oral stage) is an incorporative one: The child receives and feels accepted, thereby learning to be the kind of person who can accept from others. Later, sense impressions are received through hearing, seeing, and touching. "I am what I am given" is a one-sentence characterization. Some people may never learn to accept. They feel left out and become withdrawn. Other manifestations of mistrust could be a resignation to a view of life as chance or fate, or a tendency toward addictions of various kinds.

The child does not always perceive nurturing in the same way as it is offered by the adult. Some children are easier to nurture than others. Nor do adults realize some of the unconscious factors in the nurturing they offer. How often have parents remarked that their infant seems to know when they are preparing to go out for the evening! It would be careless psychologizing to assume that the withdrawn adult must have been shown little warmth in infancy. This is important to remember because parents more often feel guilty for what they think they have neglected than satisfied with what they have offered. We must realize that stages are *descriptive:* they are neither prescriptive nor necessarily normative.

The importance of faith and trust in human development is indicated by these words of Erikson's:

> It is not the psychologist's job to decide whether religion should or should not be confessed and practiced in particular words or rituals. Rather the psychological observer must ask whether or not in any area under observation religion and tradition are living psychological forces creating the kind of faith and conviction which permeates a parent's personality and thus reinforces the child's basic trust in the world's trustworthiness. . . .
>
> Whosoever says he has religion must derive a faith from it which is transmitted to infants in the form of basic trust; whosoever claims that he does not need religion must derive such basic faith from elsewhere.[3]

Faith and *trust* are religious words given theological meaning from a biblical context. Faith, in Christian teaching, is a reaching out toward God in confidence that through all things God will work for good to those who love him. Trust is a sense of assurance that God will do what has been promised. Faith is a leap beyond the self that results in a sense of security within the self. The two are closely bound. Through faith people are enabled to trust their whole lives into the care of God. Faith is, as Martin Luther affirmed, a gift of God, but it is freely offered. Trust is the human response to love. To those who believe that God, as creator and redeemer, loves each person with no regard as to who one is or how one acts, loving trust is the response to God's love.

The possibilities of this stage in infant development are a serious matter to the religious community. It becomes apparent that children will develop a basic trust in themselves, others, and God through living with adults who trust themselves, other people, and God. The church, through clergy and laity, will need to help strengthen the faith of its members in many ways, with a particular focus on the needs of parents and others who bear responsibility for the nurturing of children. Only when their own faith is enriched and deepened can they have the quiet confidence that is conveyed in unconscious ways to a child. The church also should be the kind of community that gives people opportunities to grow in mutual trust through the relationships they have with one another. It should be a community that bears witness to the trustwortiness of God, affirming this by word and deed, and thereby giving support to parents and other teachers.

When the church decides to care for infants, the conditions that make for trust must be present. The nursery is not simply any place in which babies are left in order that parents may attend worship or other events. It should be the kind of room that brings reassurance to parents and children: clean, attractive, comfortable, and quiet. The person in charge should be one who is dependably present before the first child arrives, and whose being radiates confidence. Those who care for infants must love children, responding to the winsome charm of their helplessness. The child will respond positively, sensing that discomfort will be assuaged and hunger satisfied. Each will know that in a situation of distress the parent will be called and that in any event, parents will return within a reasonable time. When infants are left fretful, with a vague feeling of abandonment, they are learning that they cannot trust the situation. People in the church are not caring about them.

This is the first step in the religious education of the child.

The Toddler (About the Second and Third Years): Autonomy vs. Shame and Doubt

The toddler is developing autonomy, to the pride and dismay of the family. The child has found a voice and learned the word *no*. Precarious situations develop from the combination of increasing locomotion, developing muscular coordination, and a consuming curiosity. Toddlers can get around, they are aware of self, siblings, and other persons in the environment. The child is learning boundaries and limitations, and this is the beginning of the ability to make decisions. Wise mothers do not ask, "Will you have a cookie?" but "Which cookie will you have?" In some cultures this age becomes the occasion for toilet-training, signifying control, cleanliness, and scheduling—all values in that society. In other cultures the process may be more casual and less emotion-laden. Where grandparents or other children care for the little ones, the authority of the parent is less likely to become a struggle of wills.

Holding and letting go become keynotes of autonomy. Either may be positive; either may be destructive. Holding may mean caring for, or confining. Letting go may mean giving freedom, or destroying. When the parent enfolds the crying toddler who has been hurt, this is perceived as caring. When the crying child is angry, this holding may be perceived as confinement; the child then wants to be let go. Children, too, act upon these two meanings. I watched a little girl play with a newly acquired stuffed animal, turning it, stroking it, examining it. In another mood she might squeeze it, put it in a box, or in some other way try to confine it. To let go might be to give the child freedom to run around the room, but for other children, sadly, it may indicate indifference or carelessness. So when a child lets go of a toy, this may be a desire to share its own freedom, or it may be a casting aside.

A child needs to learn how to channel these impulses lest they be turned against the self or others. A person who has been overcontrolled finds self-identity threatened and begins to doubt the self. The lessening of self-esteem brings self-consciousness and a sense of shame; hence the need for "face-saving." For some people, the sense of shame may lead to compulsive behavior that brings reassurance. Others compensate for seemingly unrealistic demands made upon them by acting as they wish but doing so when unseen. In order to develop autonomy, children need both firmness and tolerance.

Because Christianity is a religion of law and grace, the theological implications of the toddler stage are pertinent. It has been suggested that the church does not really want persons to be autonomous. Leaders and followers make the pattern; shepherd and flock is one image. This is an oversimplification. Leaving the question of control and freedom among adults, one may ask how this stage affects the nursery class.

There needs to be a balance between order and disorder. When toys are in use, the room may look disorderly to the visiting adult; in fact, it denotes purposive play. At the end of a session, children and teachers together will put it in order. Decisions as to the use of toys and equipment ("Where would you like to begin this morning?") can usually be made by each child, although some need encouragement. Decisions about respect for other children, carefulness with the equipment, or the time for closing the session need to be made by adults. This gives children security in knowing that they will be protected. The use of freedom is learned, and wise teachers watch each child's development. The ability to resolve conflict is also learned, and adult intervention is essential with children at this age.

If you are nurturing a child to become an autonomous person, you will rejoice when the child says *no* to you as well as when the reply is *yes.* Opportunities for choice become important. Observe carefully when letting go means knocking down the wall of blocks. It could serve a good purpose at that moment, or it could become a destructive habit. Observe when a child clutches at another to see whether this denotes affection or a need to confine.

With two- and three-year-olds you are trying to provide an environment that says, "God made you a person who can will and do. We want to help you learn good uses for *no* and *yes.*" Thus teachers assist children by both controlling and freeing, so that they may experience rules as good and comfortable and at the same time feel able to assert individual needs. The grace of God is shown through relationships. Flexibility rather than rigidity is an expression of real religious community. Only adults who are flexible can make this kind of environment for little children. Others would do better work elsewhere in the life of the church.

Kindergarten (About the Fourth and Fifth Years):
Initiative vs. Guilt

The four- or five-year-old is an independent person, persistently asking questions but not always concerned about the answers. Children of this age form friendships beyond the family circle in neighborhood, kindergarten, and church. A well-developed imagination finds outlets in daydreams, tall stories, and fantasy; in books, records, or television. "What kind of person am I?" this child asks, and finds identification through parental figures. This has been called by Erikson the *intrusive mode.* The child does not hesitate to attack people physically, constantly intrudes with questions and comments, pushes, runs, and explores.

The task at this age is to develop initiative. While Erikson noted that boys feel closer to mother and girls to father, each in a way dreaming of "marrying" this important person, it is also noticeable that children begin to identify with a near adult of the same sex. Our culture has encouraged a distinct separation of roles. Both schools and homes ply four- and five-year-olds with "appropriate" toys. The aggressive behavior of boys may be admonished—but in admiring tones— while girls win approval by behaving in quiet ways. At kindergarten boys may be shunted from the housekeeping corner to the blocks, while girls are encouraged to become proficient housekeepers. At a time when young adults are insisting on interchangeable roles, it can be expected that their children, male or female, will be exposed to housekeeping and blockbuilding, given doctor's kits and nurse's kits, and thereby will identify with parents who are widening their own role choices.

As a consequence of close identity with the parent of the same sex and deep affection for the parent of the opposite sex, the child develops feelings of jealousy and rivalry but is too small to express these except as anger. These loved adults on whom a child is so dependent, who are so powerful and sometimes unpredictable, evoke ambivalent feelings and provoke a sense of guilt. It is important that children feel assured of the continuing affection and care of the elders, their acceptance of this hostility-with-love, and grow up not with buried guilt but with a strengthened sense of initiative.

At this age the child's conscience is also established, basically as obedience to the parents. Conscience sets boundaries for initiative. If the rules are lenient, the child may become uncertain how to act in situations requiring moral decision. If they are rigid, the child becomes unable to respond freely. Such a child could become the overly conscientious adult who expects to be valued only for accomplishment, tirelessly performing work that may be expected to bring recognition and, in consequence, valuing other people only in terms of their performance. The child who attempts to follow parental dictates but observes that parents disregard the same rules will resent the double standard. This adds to the conflict already inherent in an age of developing initiative.

The church has shared societal values in this respect. The person who performs the most church work is frequently the most valued. Yet the example set for us is that Jesus valued persons for who they were—and frequently in spite of—how they acted. Bring this insight to the church kindergarten. It is easy to give approval to quiet children who relate easily to others and perform well; they assure the teacher of having done well. Yet everyone has suffered from some overbearing person or situation insisting on impossible goals. Lighten the conscience of the small child. It is not right to hit another child, but it is all right to feel angry. Show the child ways of expressing anger without hurting other people. Give help to see the possible reason for anger. Encourage alternative ways of action for the child whose only security seems to lie in trying to do tasks perfectly. Painting can be messy, but water is for washing up. Puzzles won't always come out perfectly. Blocks don't always balance, but one can develop skill in using them.

Then there is the matter of identification. This is the pleasure of being oneself, and children achieve it when they are encouraged to range freely among activities and materials. Being human is a quality needed today: gentleness and strength, giving and receiving, being active and being quiet —for men and women, boys and girls. The church nursery class should have as teachers men and women who illustrate for young children the meaning of scripture: "In the image of God he created him; male and female he created them" (Gen.1:27). Remember also the words of the apostle Paul, "There is neither male nor female; for you are all one in Christ Jesus" (Gal. 3:28).

André Godin, a Belgian psychologist, made a study of the relationship between adults' understandings of God the Father and feelings toward their own fathers.[4] Men and women translated the words *Father God* differently, for fathers traditionally have treated daughters protectively and encouraged sons to be strong. People tended to image God after the preferred parent and to reflect both an idealized parent and childhood aggression toward parents. A spiritual task of adulthood is to free the understanding of God from parental imaging. Whenever the word *Father* is used with reference to God, adults should be aware that children can only understand this in terms of the father they know. Usually the father is basically a kind and very human person, though for some he may be an angry, even cruel, person. Others remember no father, or one who is seen infrequently. Nevertheless, the address to God as Father is written into the Bible, particularly for Christians in the address of the Lord's Prayer. The word describes some of the ways God acts. "As a father pities his children, so the Lord pities those who fear him" (Ps. 103:13); "Have we not all one father? Did not one God create us?" (Mal. 2:10). Jesus pictured the forgiving father (Luke 15) and the father who gives bread to his children (Luke 11:11). Like a parent—mother or father—God fed his people, guided them, corrected them, forgave them, and never forsook them. Human fathers are not perfect, but the child can find security in the assurance that the divine parent is always dependable.

The Elementary Age (About the Sixth to Twelfth Years): Industry vs. Inferiority

At about age six children are introduced to the skills necessary for adult functioning, developing what Erikson calls a sense of industry. In Western cultures this involves reading, written expression, and number work. This activity is in harmony with the child's developing experiences, curiosity, and pleasure in accomplishment. Children work hard, and play is part of the work. This stage is the final period of childhood, as long in duration as the three earlier periods. Erikson says:

> One might say that personality at the first stage crystalizes around the conviction "I am what I am given," and that of the second, "I am what I will." The third can be characterized by "I am what I can imagine I will be." We must now approach the fourth, "I am what I learn."[5]

Play is part of this work insofar as skills are developed; it differs from preschool play, in which imitation and socialization are the accomplishments. The child plays in order to accomplish, whether in games of physical skill or thought, or those that test knowledge. The satisfaction comes from knowing that the work is well done, as validated in the approval of parent or teacher and in recognition by peers. The child also derives satisfaction from the practice that leads toward competence. It is frustrating to be unable to read when everyone else can do so, to make continued mistakes in arithmetic, and always to see corrections on written work. Thus the opposite of *industry* becomes *inferiority*. It is sad when a small child can feel that there is no way of pleasing the parent, no way of winning approval from the teacher. Such a child becomes discouraged and gives up the unequal struggle, never acquiring the enjoyment of work or the satisfaction of doing well.

The task for the teacher is to find out how each child is motivated. Sometimes permitting individual initiative produces a learning situation, and at other times a set task is a stimulus. Whether learning is play or work, an extension of early childhood or a foretaste of maturity, should not be a matter of pendulum swings in educational theory but rather an adaptation to the needs of each situation. In serious application to learning tasks, a child learns to live within boundaries and to accept self-restraints in the interest of achieving a goal. The basic thrust of the elementary stage is social accomplishment, but the outcome is crucial for the whole life of an individual within a society. Erikson warns that sometimes a culture can block development by the stereotypes under which it operates. He says, "When a child begins to feel that it is the color of his skin, the background of his parents, or the cost of his clothes rather than his wish and his will to learn which will decide his social worth, lasting harm may ensue for the sense of identity."[6]

In its educational work the church must take seriously the need for a sense of accomplishment that children have between the ages of six and twelve. More teachers are involved with this age group, more parents are transporting children to and from church, more rooms, equipment, curricular materials, and money are involved here than with any other group of people within the church. What kind of assurance do these children have of developing skills and accomplishing learning?

Some churches, perhaps whole denominations, have a well-defined tradition and body of teaching material, usually biblical, which can be communicated to children. Through stories, games, writing, and other specific methods, children can learn the outline of the biblical tradition and its application to personal life as understood by the church. Teachers concerned about children's religious growth provide the needed emotional environment. Parents and teachers who share this tradition reinforce the children's learning. The rewards may be tangible, such as points given for learning and a gift at the end of the year. They are also intangible: the satisfaction of accomplishment.

Other Christian groups are less specific in what they want taught; parents, teachers, or clergy do not see education in terms of such concrete learning. The child may enjoy the environment of the class, but by fourth or fifth grade the lack of substance has become frustrating. This is one reason for the discipline problems reported by teachers in upper elementary grades. The child who has learned how to grasp meaning through silent reading does not want to read aloud sentences from a book in rotation. The child who has used inductive skills for solving problems in science class does not want to answer what he or she would consider "dumb" questions. The child who has heard all kinds of questions welcomed is made uncomfortable by a teacher who is upset when children ask any question that does not have a definite answer.

The significance of the elementary stage to religious development is that the church needs to devise ways of using the growing child's skills and knowledge for the furtherance of religious understanding. Too many church school sessions, whether held on Sunday, weekday, or during vacation time, are staffed by volunteers who decry their own limitations yet do not take the steps necessary to become informed teachers. They derive satisfaction from having done a favor for the pastor who was desperate for help and seem not to realize that both their own egos and those of the children would be better sustained by some good hard work. Children want to be motivated by having their curiosity aroused and interest directed; want to use new-found skills in reading, investigation, research, and experiment, as well as in play-acting, writing, conversation, games, and construction work. But methods alone can be clever and empty; they are only media for the communication of learning.

A section that began by focusing on the psychological development of children ends by discussing the more tangible outcomes of learning. Writing is inevitably linear, giving the reader a feeling of precise chronological development. Child development proceeds in several directions simultaneously, and each direction has its own pace. Child psychologists, speaking of "holistic learning," have noted that the human organism tends toward what they term *homeostasis,* a balance in which all elements coexist comfortably. Stages must be described consecutively, but in the living child they develop integrally, although at an individual rate. The specific descriptions of child development vary with each researcher. Already assertions about role development are being called into question. What parents and teachers learn is the direction of development. These insights can be helpful in guiding the religious nurturing of children.

CHAPTER 2

The Child

Thinks

T H E development of cognitive learning has been studied extensively by the Swiss psychologist Jean Piaget. By *cognitive learning* he means intellectual development, the ability to think, express ideas, figure out the *why,* and discuss. From careful observation of his own three children and the study of groups of children at school and play, Piaget acquired the data for some basic theses, which he applied in his books to many areas of children's learning.

Piaget understands intellectual development to go through several stages. These are not mechanical; the length of time a child stays in one stage and the adaptation to the next stage will differ with individuals, but the process will continue. No child jumps from stage one to stage three. No child regresses from stage two to stage one. The organization of thought within the brain proceeds in an orderly way. The structures change systematically as the child develops, but the functions of organization and adaptation remain. The change in structures is developmental. Piaget's studies remind us to be careful to know where each child is developmentally when we plan for religious education at each age. This is why his theories of the development of thought processes need to be studied by all people involved in the process of teaching about history, miracle, beliefs, and the Bible.

The Sensorimotor Stage: Birth to Age Two

From birth to about the age of two, a child learns through a feeling-action response to the external environment, human and physical. The newborn begins in a reflex stage, using instinctual drives and emotions, where each action, such as sucking, turning the head, or moving legs and arms, is an immediate response to a need or an external stimulus. Motor habits are developed. Then the infant organizes actions and perceptions in a way that indicates what adults would call learning. Finally, the child shows the development of sensorimotor intelligence by looking for objects or playing hide-and-seek with a parent. The cognitive development during these two years, before the beginning of the use of language is, says Piaget, "a miniature Copernican revolution."[1]

This child is in a self-centered stage by the simple fact of having difficulty in differentiating the self from others in the environment. The increasing ability to sense, feel, act, and move about makes possible this separation and the possibility of seeing others as separate entities to whom the child can relate.

This is the age at which children are in the toddlers' group at church, needing people who will stimulate their development by their loving presence, providing toys and equipment through which they may explore their wonderful world.

The Preoperational Stage: Ages Two to Seven

When the child can speak, a second stage has been reached, characterizing the early childhood years from two to seven. Now there is the possibility of speaking to others and therefore of socialization. Words can be internalized to become thought. The child can reflect on behavior. Actions also can become internalized. This means that the child can develop relationships with and feelings about other people. Where the infant's task was to relate to and understand the physical environment, the young child's task is that of socialization. This decreases the egocentricity so characteristic of infancy and makes possible more objective responses to situations. The child talks constantly: to adults, to other children, and to the self. There is the possibility of play with others. Thinking is intuitive. Asked why something is so, the child will say "Because it is," or "It always has been," or "I don't know." To the child at this age, actions are not reversible. If something is, no further reasons are needed. Ideas are stated successively, and there is no attempt to build on one statement to develop a complex idea. It is an age of concrete, practical intelligence, of centering on the details of an event without fully grasping its wholeness.

This is the age when the church nursery and kindergarten can provide an environment in which to explore relationships. Teachers and other children interacting in play and conversation assist in the process. Equipment for playing house, building, and locomotion are the means through which children learn how to respond to situations with less egocentricity than in infancy.

The Concrete-Operational Stage: Ages Seven to Twelve

This stage brings a substantial cognitive development. Children are able clearly to differentiate the self from others and to engage in cooperative endeavors. They understand relationships between objects. Intuition has become transformed into operational thinking in concrete situations. For example, a child is shown two sticks of identical length lying on a table. When one is moved slightly to the right of the other (but still parallel) the preschool child will say that one is longer than the other. The seven- to eight-year-old will know that they are still the same size and that only the position has been changed. This illustrates the principle of reversibility. Older children understand that the place of the sticks can be changed without changing their size.

Small children who observe identical amounts of water poured into a tall beaker and into a wide container will insist that the former contains more water because the liquid stands higher in the container. However, children at the concrete-operational stage have developed the principle of conservation; they are able to understand that the volume can be the same when the shape changes.

The concrete-operational stage is the time when concrete learning should characterize religious education classes: stories from biblical and childhood situations, experiences that help children remember and understand the stories.

The Formal-Operational Stage: Beyond Age Twelve

At the age of about eleven or twelve the child begins to enter the stage of abstract thinking. This is the ability to conceptualize, what adults do when they speak of *thinking*. Only at adolescence and into adulthood can a person construct theories and systems, and become able to philosophize or theologize. This is hypothetical and deductive thinking. Reflection becomes possible, and ideas become exciting. Thinking can become propositional: The learner can see the possible as well as the immediate; what might be as well as what is. These are the years in which the church should be helping children interpret biblical material. Why did Amos speak as he did to his people? What is the Sermon on the Mount saying to us today? A new world of activity is opened.

Understanding the Terms

There are a number of terms to explain the flow of Piaget's developmental stages. The child incorporates new learning through the processes of assimilation and accommodation. *Assimilation* means that the child internalizes new learning and can begin to use it; it has become part of the self and can be used for building new cognitive structures. *Accommodation* is the process by which the child modifies thought processes or understandings in order to incorporate new learning. The use of these two processes, called *adaptation,* makes possible the maintenance of equilibrium while new structures are developing. At the end of each stage there comes a transitional time when the child's responses come closer to those characteristic of the next stage.

Ways in which these stages and terms pertain to religious education will be discussed more fully in Chapters 5 and 11, when the findings of David Elkind and Ronald Goldman are considered. Here, however, reference can be made to an understanding of a biblical story. Seeing a picture of people in long flowing robes and boats of quite different construction from those known locally, the child accommodates his or her thought patterns to this reality and thinks, "This isn't how I know people to dress, but the picture says that people have looked like that." At a later age, the child will perceive that people have similar needs wherever or whenever they live. Told that the Bible says, "When I lie down I will rest in peace, for only you make me sleep in safety," the child receives reassurance in a life experience—that is, of going to bed in the dark—and assimilates this for comfort.

Piaget views the human organism as constantly in action. Action is a response to needs, and needs are the motivation for action. A need indicates disequilibrium, which is uncomfortable. When the need is satisfied, equilibrium is established. As the child develops, the adaptive processes of accommodation and assimilation are repeated to bring the self into a new equilibrium in order to move toward the next stage. Each stage is the substructure on which the next is built. At each stage the modes of operation characteristic of an earlier stage are transformed to express new modes of learning. There is a certain permanence throughout constant change. The person is the same person, developing almost imperceptibly, except as one views the changes across a span of years.

Piaget has applied this basic definition of the structures of cognitive learning to specific areas in a series of books.[2] Following are some of the concepts discussed in these books that have implications for the religious education of children.

The Concept of Time

The infant has no understanding of time as duration, much less of time as past-present-future. In the rhythm of infancy the moment is the important concept, and the child responds to each immediate need. There may be a vague feeling of duration. The infant evidences "practical" time; that is, when a sound is heard, the head is turned. Only slowly does the infant develop even a sense of *before* and *after.* When mother leaves the room, she is gone. But a time comes when, if a person hides behind a screen, the child will look for a reappearance. Children in the preoperational stage do not separate time and velocity in space, cannot see vehicles traveling a specific distance at varying rates of speed as traveling at different time-spans. Only during the concrete-operational stage (beginning at age six or seven) do children begin to understand "operational" time. "Next Saturday" (spoken on Monday) may be less exact a time span than it would be to adults, but the child can differentiate it from tomorrow. Psychological time, the "sense" of time, follows the same cognitive constructs. As Piaget states, "Grasping time is tantamount to freeing oneself from the present, to transcending space by a mobile effort, i.e., by reversible operations."[3]

Children in the preoperational and concrete-operational stages, do not begin to deal with time as the sense of history, but too often in religious education it is taken for granted that teaching about the distant past is possible. Piaget's study of the child's developing sense of time implies that, while children may understand stories of people who lived in the past in terms of human experience, they cannot grasp the span of biblical history as time. Events in series can be learned by older children (Abraham lived before David, who lived before Paul) but *ancient* and *modern* have no meaning, and *a long time ago* might mean last year. Learning biblical stories in chronological order, however, may help children more easily unscramble events and characters when they are old enough to grasp the concept of history. Later they will be able to assimilate a period of history in its setting, such as the Exodus or the beginning of the church in the Book of Acts. Finally, at age eleven–twelve, children can feel the sweep of biblical history.

The Child's Conception of the World

The conception of the world is concerned with the content rather than the structure of children's thinking. In doing his research, Piaget used the spontaneous questions of children instead of directing questions to them.[4] He outlines three stages. In the stage of realism (ages five to six) the child does not discriminate clearly between psychological and physical events. Experiences and objective reality are confused. Dreams (which are experiences) are believed to be substantial (that is, events.) A stone, although it cannot move of itself, can have feelings. Conversely, in the stage of animism (ages seven to eight) the child endows with consciousness only those objects which can move, such as a bicycle. In the stage of artificialism (ages nine to ten) the child believes that physical phenomena are made by humans to serve human purposes. The light exists so that we can go to bed; the sun shines to make us warm. Children in the stage of artificialism also believe that everything has been made, either by God or by humans. Mountains are made; so are lakes and cities (as a matter of fact some lakes *are* made!). Children are made. Children of nine or ten have no trouble accepting the idea that God ordered into being the earth, sun, and moon, or fashioned a man from the earth. Parents and teachers need to be aware of children's thought structures with reference to their own theological interpretation of biblical materials, for it should give clues as to the age at which to introduce materials. It is only at the end of the concrete-operational stage that children see external realities as having their own reason for being. The representation of reality then includes past, present, and future. Here, as in so many other areas, the child's ability to transcend the self and to develop beyond self-centeredness is a pivotal factor. The child must be able to differentiate the self fully from the external world.

What does this say for religious education? Because of the propensity of children before the age of seven or eight to attribute magical properties and explanations to marvelous events, teachers and curriculum writers should be careful as to what biblical material is selected for preschool and early elementary age children. Christianity is not a religion of magic, and we do not want children to confuse magic (forcing divine power through human agency) with miracle (the mighty acts of God). We do not want them to view Jesus as a magician; at this stage, telling of how he walked on the water or changed water into wine could do this. By trying to do too much too soon, we can easily cause the learner to have a distorted view of the biblical truth. It could interfere with later understanding of biblical narratives.

Play, Dreams, and Imitation

The infant imitates actions. Learning occurs by imitating people—their smiles, the way they form words, or the way they move their hands. Some actions are symbolic, as when the young child, before learning to speak, forms with his or her hands the shape of the desired object that has disappeared. The earliest form of play is exercise for the infant who moves arms, legs, and head. "Pretend" and "make believe" are forms of symbolic play where one object substitutes for another. Piaget feels that the content of the dreams of children aged four to six is similar to the symbols used in games.[5] Games combine both imitation and play as young children reenact family activities. It is only when the child enters the stage of concrete-operational thinking that games with rules emerge. Then the outlines become clear, and each child engaged in the game must understand how it is played, the rewards, and the penalties. It is all very logical—and concrete.

Games and other forms of play have long been used in religious education. Most observers recognize the symbolism within the kindergarten or nursery child's "free" activities. Through play children can transform the real into whatever they desire. The use of games has become popular at all ages as a way by which the learner can identify with other people in a learning situation. This might be the housekeeping corner in the kindergarten, or games of social awareness for adults. Drama, including the use of various forms of puppets and role-playing, is frequently used in the church school from the age of six.

The child, however, does not recognize the symbols used, taught, and understood by adults. Piaget writes about the development of the child's own symbol system. What we learn from his study is to be aware of children's symbols as their way of reenacting experience. Children's construction of symbolic actions does not guarantee that children will understand the symbols that they see in churches, or understand the symbolic words and rites that are so important an expression of religious experience. Where symbols are pictures of events or where word and picture coincide, there can be meaning. The cross can have meaning as event. We say, "The cross tells us in a special way about God's love." It says that love is greater than any hurt or wrong. Where the symbol replaces abstract definition, the child will not understand it, as with symbols for the trinity or most of the symbols for Christ. The development of the understanding of religious symbol follows the same structures as does any other kind of learning.

The Origin of the Idea of Chance

The origin of the idea of chance brings the child's thinking from the possible to the necessary. To the child in the preoperational stage anything can happen; "Can it happen?" or "Must it happen?" evoke the same positive response. For example, when a game of chance was played and the children observed that counters thrown on a board would turn up some with crosses and some with circles (heads or tails), they accepted this fact. However, when a substitute set of counters was thrown and all turned up with crosses, younger children raised not a question. It was only those in the concrete-operational stage, capable of some deductive reasoning, who were sure that something must have been different from the start They understood that the idea of chance implied more than one possibility. Piaget says of children at the preoperational stage:

> Since they lack deductive operations and the notion of chance, everything for them is, in differing degrees, miraculous. It is only when we have a rational mind that the question of miracle is posed because it is contrary both to natural regularities and to fortuitous fluctuations. For the ancients, on the contrary, miracle (in the etymological meaning of "marvel" or "wonder") was a natural thing, and for the primitive, everything is, in fact, a miracle. It is precisely the same reaction which our subjects of the first stage present, and for the same reasons.[6]

Only by concrete thinking can the child accept as fact the reality of chance. Then there can be a clear differentiation between the necessary and the possible.

This study by Piaget is another indication to those concerned with the religious education of children that young children are aware of the marvelous differently than older children are—they will not even realize that an event is unusual. The mighty works of the Bible that were, and can be, a source of amazement to adults are taken matter-of-factly by the small child. Unless you want the unusual to seem usual and the supernatural to seem natural, remember that there is a time for everything. The time to tell of miracle is not in kindergarten.

Language and Thought of the Child

Piaget began by studying for one month the questions of two six-year-old children in school.[7] Then his studies moved to younger children, exploring the development of the use of language. His conclusions are that, in the preoperational stage, when children are first becoming fluent in the use of language, they talk more to themselves than to their peers. This egocentric speech Piaget calls *collective monologues.* At the age of six the child is learning how to use speech for communication, and it becomes a socializing factor. Children learn how to explain something to one another. They learn how to carry on conversations in which they are really listening and responding to each other.

"Why" questions are only slowly understood. *Because* is a word young children do not know how to use. They use *then,* which ignores the casual factor. The connective *although* is not comprehended until the ages of eleven or twelve. Even then children have trouble understanding the explanation of a biblical proverb. This is because parallel reasoning is not clear to them. Self-centeredness (child egocentrism) is a basic factor in the young child's inability to explore *why.* The developing process of socialization, helped by the development of language, makes it increasingly possible to go beyond the self to explore such questions.

There are three types of *why* used by children up to the age of seven. There is the *why* of causal explanation. It asks for an interpretation of a statement that gives assurance that something really is as they see it. "Why does a tree have leaves?" would suggest to an adult an answer that explains the need for roots or sunshine. The child may simply expect an answer such as "to give us shade." The *why* of motivation (Why are you going away?) asks about psychological factors. The *why* of justification implies that there are customs and rules governing events. These "why" questions are not philosophical but practical. The children want to understand. One asks, "Why are the gowns black in some churches and colored in others?" By the age of eight the children are looking for logical justification; they can think in concrete operational terms. Save the philosophical questions. The children will not be ready until the age of twelve or later.

Piaget's findings must be taken seriously in religious education. Many teachers find it difficult to believe that children's questions do not have some profound motivation. The teacher feels rewarded when a five-year-old asks "Who is God?" or "Where is God?" but the children are not asking theological (that is abstract operational) questions. They want concrete answers. The answer to the question "Who is God?" is not to the effect that God is everywhere, powerful, or loving, but that God is one whom we cannot see yet who loves us and cares for us through people and through the world (rain, sun, food). "Where is God?" is a question not about heaven or infinity but about the presence of God. A question about who Jesus is does not demand a christological explanation. The dress of people in biblical illustrations is so far removed from anything present-day children see that even assuring them that Jesus was a person who lived a long time ago in a faraway country fixes his humanity in mind. When teachers say that Jesus is "here," and again that God is "here," this may cause confusion in the child's mind, but it is part of the Christian understanding of the Easter faith.

We never fully know, except by their questions, when children are puzzled or when they accept adult statements as words to be sorted out later. Important for the realistic appraisal of learning is the adult understanding that children will want concrete answers. The young child's questions are not nearly so difficult to answer as some teachers would believe. For this reason, it is important to try to hear what the child is really saying instead of translating the child's question into adult terms. Think of the stage of cognitive development, then try to figure out the kind of answer the question seeks.

Moral Judgment and the Child

Moral Judgment and the Child is Piaget's book that most directly affects the understanding of the religious education of children.[8] Two basic areas are discussed: the rules of the games children play, and the way in which adults carry out justice. Watching children playing marbles, Piaget noticed that no rules were observed by the preschool children playing together. Rules were considered inviolable, as if from some divine source, by the six- to eight-year-olds, although they were frequently broken in the children's strivings to participate in this group activity. Until the ages of eleven or twelve there was still inconsistency in the way rules were kept; however, there was also a developing interest in codifying them and at the same time agreement to modification and constant revision.

Piaget also studied the child's developing sense of justice.

In one story, a little boy, responding to the call to dinner, bumps into a chair behind a door and knocks against a tray on which are fifteen cups, all of which break. Another child reaches into a cupboard to get jam while his mother is out, and knocks over one cup that breaks. The question is: Who deserves more punishment? "The boy who broke fifteen cups," say children at about age seven. "The boy who broke one cup," say children at about age nine. Younger children (ages four to eight) were expecting objective (heteronomous) justice—the punishment should fit the amount of damage. Older children (ages eight to twelve) were asking for subjective (autonomous) justice— intention was the pivotal factor. The first child was being obedient and did not mean to break the cups. The second child was being disobedient.

In questions seeking to elicit the child's understanding of a lie, it was found that preschool children see lies as "naughty words," that is, words they were taught not to use. Between the ages of six and ten, children define a lie as any untrue statement. Although they know the difference between intention and action (even preschool children may understand this), they do not make a clear differentiation when questioned on the subject. By the age of ten, children are beginning to perceive clearly and to be able to explain to others that only an untrue statement that was meant to deceive is a lie. Intention becomes important as age increases. Up to age ten, most children say that a lie is wrong if it is discovered and punished. Beyond this age, children understand that lying is punished because it is wrong.

In another context Piaget drew the conclusion that preschool children accept punishment as just when it comes from an authority figure. Children up to age seven think it should "fit the crime"; from the ages of eight to ten, about half would agree to this, while the rest think that punishment should reflect the intention of the person who did wrong.

After the age of ten, children regard as fair a punishment that takes into account whether or not the person acting meant to break a rule. In Piaget's terminology, children below the age of ten see moral absolutes ("moral realism"); after that they develop a "morality of cooperation."[11]

Think of these findings with reference to how children are taught the meaning of Christian living, of law and grace, of judgment and forgiveness. The youngest children expect the penalty to fit the damage done and accept the judgment of the adult. Teachers and parents want to think first of the child's needs. This does not mean that you use a child's estimate, only that you recognize how children feel. Children accept your generous decisions even when they do not fully understand. It will be time before they grasp the meaning of grace. They are harder on each other (and sometimes on themselves) than you would be. The parables of grace receive curious interpretations. Most children will feel that in forgiving the prodigal son, the father was being unfair to the son who had stayed at home. Why was he not rewarded for doing what his father wanted? When told the story of the workers in the vineyard who came at different times but were given the same wages at the end of the day, some children will respond, "That's just the way it is at home. My brother (or sister) always gets more than I do." They can appreciate grace for themselves—but not for others. When you are trying to be fair, be sure you are aware of the difference between their understanding of that word and yours. They understand love, but justice, in an adult sense, is beyond them.

Affective learning, that is, learning through feelings, is not treated in any specific way by Piaget but there are references to it in several of his books. Although his primary concern is with cognitive development, Piaget realizes that affective development is part of the same child. There is no such thing as a purely intellectual action. Motives reveal affectivity. The interest and curiosity of a child affect learning. Values become differentiated in the course of development, and the child's self-evaluation is one factor in value clarification. It is in the areas of mutual respect, justice, moral feelings, and the development of the will that Piaget seeks the affective life. He does not give us many clues for understanding interpersonal relationships. In these studies, one sees most frequently the interaction of a single child and adult, or that of children of the same age group. While the development of relationships is another whole field, in which others have pioneered, the far-reaching contribution of Jean Piaget to the understanding of the child's cognitive development does have important implications for religious education.

CHAPTER 3

The Child
—————————

Feels
—————————

C H I L D R E N have feelings. We know this, but we may not always use the knowledge. At home, where they spend much of their time, young children express spontaneous feelings. Sometimes they get what they want by doing so. As they grow, some are taught to channel feelings in various ways; others are told to hide them.

When children come to church school they have already learned ways of handling feelings, but they need to try these out in a new situation. They want to know how people will react. All the years they are in churches they will be finding out how people react to feelings and how they think these should be handled.

Affection

Human beings are born with feelings.[1] The newborn infant knows pleasant and unpleasant feelings. Affection soon develops toward nurturing persons, especially those who feed and change the infant. The warmth of a presence and the soothing sound of a voice give the first feelings of security in a strange world. Here are the beginnings of the basic trust mentioned earlier. The very young child reaches out lovingly toward others, denoting that feeling with a smile or gesture. When a child can walk, the world begins to expand, other people are drawn into the child's orbit. To give and receive pleasure evokes feelings of affection. The child shows this toward other people: brothers and sisters, grandparents or other relatives who appear frequently, close family friends or neighbors who live nearby.

As the circle of acquaintances enlarges, the child develops friends among nearby children. Affection is shown in the way they play together and in the sharing (however imperfect) of toys. If the family has evoked warmth, by the time the child reaches church school age he or she spontaneously reaches out toward new friends, both adults and other children. That is why it is important that those who work with young children be people who can easily express warmth. The nursery and kindergarten can be important in the growth of children. Wise teachers are sensitive to when a child needs the comfort of a pat or an encircling arm, and when a smile from a distance is all that child is ready to accept. The most satisfying experiences for teachers of children come when their patient, restrained overtures evoke positive feelings in response.

At the elementary age, children may be less spontaneous in showing affection than they were when younger. Good will exuded in a relaxed, expansive manner by their enthusiasm for whatever they are doing tells the teacher that the children feel basically good toward other people. They show generosity and willingness to assist other children, when necessary; they do not hold resentments and indicate no need to "prove" either their own affection for others or that of others for them.

It should be remembered that children develop deep affection for animal pets of all kinds, and that loss of a pet is a cause for sorrow. Little children also develop an affection for objects such as favorite dolls or stuffed animals. When this becomes more important than affection for persons, it would seem that a child prefers to love where there is security and a predictable response rather than risk the uncertainties of the give-and-take with humans whose feelings might seem to change suddenly. Children who have few human contacts for affection may need objects, but these can never fully replace the need for nurturing persons.

Growing out of the ability to give and receive affection are feelings of joy, pleasure, delight, and even happiness. These words are used descriptively rather than definitively, each has figured in philosophical systems and this is not the place to differentiate among them. Given that all persons have "high" and "low" days, there is a basic orientation toward life that calls it good in spite of negative events. The child with basic security accepts the bad times as part of the whole. Popular wisdom pictures this in terms of clouds and sunshine. Adults respond with immediate identification to the feelings of children. Few things give them more pleasure than to watch children expressing spontaneous joy. At the same time, many adults are quickly upset by the unhappy tears of children and hasten to try to change the mood. Children need to cry as well as to laugh; to feel unhappy as well as happy.

This balance of feelings is important, the ability to move back into equilibrium and not to experience frequent and radical changes of mood. Parents learn early in their associations with infants to distinguish among the cries of hunger, pain, discomfort, or anger.

Children feel content when their world is basically secure. When there is stability and children know that they can trust others and are trusted, they feel an inner freedom that permits them to relax. They can play spontaneously and do their best work. They can be generous in their dealings with other children and friendly toward adults.

Anger, Hostility, and Anxiety

Some negative feelings are also valid responses to human situations. These emotions need to be expressed, but they need also to be handled in ways that are not damaging to the person holding them or those toward whom they are expressed. Anger is such a feeling. The newborn, red-faced and tense, seems to feel this way. Anger is a common response to frustration. This way of meeting situations can persist for a long time. Some people never get beyond it. Learning how to control and express anger—and when to do each—is important. Such control will not come simply through the process of maturation, although the possibility for learning skills is there. The ways in which parents respond to a child's anger is important. When parents feel attacked, or feel that they have failed the child, or that they do not deserve this kind of response, they may in turn become angry. If they maintain an adult perspective, they can become aware of why the child expresses feelings this way.

Anger occurs when situations are beyond a child's control. The hungry or tired child has a low tolerance level. A child will vent wrath at an object by hitting it, even when he or she is hurt by the contact. A favorite toy may be thrown across the room. Adults tend to smile at this. When a child hits a person, this is regarded as unacceptable behavior. Yet each action is an alternative to bottling up anger. A child with such feelings needs an adult who will express understanding and make alternative suggestions.

Anger may flare suddenly and then recede, as with a tantrum. Anger, when repressed, becomes hostility. Hostility is deeper and lasts longer. It is not caused by an immediate event but builds up. A child may feel that someone else is more favored or that someone is expressing dislike. There is an uncomfortable feeling of not being accepted or not belonging, and the child's world is put out of focus. It is not a matter to be treated lightly, nor will indulgence solve it. Commands to be kind or reassurances of love are of no avail. One must try to change the child's perception of persons and situations. Remember that the child's estimate may, in fact, be correct. Children have a subtle awareness of emotional climates.

Expressing Feelings in the Church School

Children bring feelings to the church school. Teachers, who may also be parents, will be dealing with situations that may involve anger or hostility. While some children need ways of expressing aggressiveness and even hostility, others need protection from misdirected feelings. Teachers learn how to be firm but gentle so that their guidance is fair as well as kind.

Religious sanctions could be harmful. Most people know better than to inspire children with fear that God will be angry or will punish them. To suggest that God is disappointed in an erring child or desires to have only "good" children will deepen guilt feelings. Children need to deal with anger immediately and constructively. When they have reached an age where prayer becomes a turning toward God, children may find that a murmur for help tones down their anger and assists them in seeing the situation in a different perspective. This is part of the process of religious maturing. They may find that when they reflect on a day's events at bedtime, the prayer for forgiveness will help in dealing with feelings of guilt as well as turning them positively toward the future.

Story, conversation, and prayer within the church school group can bring religious insights into focus. Biblical stories recount anger that sometimes led to tragedy. Jesus taught that his followers were not to show anger. Paul, with great wisdom, said, "Do not let the sun go down on your anger" (Eph. 4:26). Yet there are occasions when controlled anger may be the only mature response to injustice or other forms of evil. Jesus was angry when he observed some people critical of him for healing a man on the Sabbath (Mark 3:5).

Older children have their own reasons for feeling hostile. They want their rights. Sometimes they are driven by a competitiveness encouraged by family, school, and community that causes them to resent those who surpass them. They envy others for their possessions. They may be jealous of those they feel are more loved or favored. Such feelings, more complicated than specific anger, can build into hostility. When one has developed some capacity for self-transcendence and some ability to reason, it is possible to see more than one side of a matter. Hostility cannot be resolved until a person recognizes that the roots are within the self and not in others.

Religious insights can help children with problems in relationships. They can begin to find ways of meeting aggressiveness, of being assertive without being destructively aggressive, when to withdraw from a situation, and when to try to intervene constructively. Biblical stories make them aware that Jesus did not turn against even those who sought his destruction. They also know that they live in a culture that is not very comfortable with such Christian counsels as loving one's enemy and turning the other cheek.

Meeting Fears and Anxiety

Fear is another emotion children feel. Newborn infants can show fear. They are helpless, and fear is a response to the unknown by those who feel vulnerable. Everything is unknown to those who have just begun to live. Being alone can seem like being abandoned. Loud noises are fearful. Big objects, strange places, and strange people cause apprehension. The infant does not realize that a person who leaves the room will return: There is no sense of time or distance. Fear may develop as the result of a frightening experience. The obvious example is that of a child who is comfortable with the family's dog but later is knocked over by a large, strange one. It may be a long process before the child can again feel comfortable when a dog approaches.

All teachers have had in class a shy child who plays alone and rarely speaks. Such children are afraid of what will happen when they trust themselves to others. They expect to be hurt, ridiculed, or left out. Older children may be afraid of giving wrong answers lest they be sharply corrected by a teacher or laughed at by other children. It is not easy to build up confidence so that such children will take risks. I refer here to "normal" children and not to those with emotional problems whose growth is a long process requiring special skills on the part of professionally trained teachers.

Teachers can deal with children's fears once they have discovered the reason for them. Most children can learn how to look with some objectivity at the cause and to learn new responses. Teachers help by their own understanding and affection as they place confidence in such children.

Anxiety is not the same as fear. It is a feeling, deep inside a person, that does not usually have a specific focus. Some people seem always to be anxious. When one difficulty is cleared up, they expect something else to happen. Some children are always anxious. There is a tenseness about them, as if they are always expecting the worst to happen. Neither words nor experiences seem to bring reassurance; they do not believe that the world can be good or that people can be trusted. Everyone feels low at times, for such is the cyclic nature of the life pattern. However, most people usually feel good about life and about themselves unless there is a specific reason for feeling otherwise. The teacher affirms this possibility by being a confident person, warm and outgoing, trustworthy, drawing anxious children into feeling more relaxed.

Quoting biblical verses will not overcome fear and anxiety in children, but it can begin a process through which a sense of security is developed. The Bible gives assurance of God's presence: He cares about you. Jesus told his hearers that God who feeds the birds and clothes the flowers will take care of people also. Jacob, far from home, dreams of the Lord as saying "I am with you and will keep you wherever you go, and will bring you back to this land" (Gen. 28:15). That was comforting to a young man fearful of the next steps. Through prayer in class and worship in the church service, children learn how to pray when alone, have their growing faith in God deepened, and become increasingly aware that they are loved by God and may respond in love. These are specific ways that teachers can help children handle fears and anxieties through the resources of Christian faith. Look up in a concordance some time the words *fear, afraid, anxious,* and see how many references there are to verses that say "Do not fear," or "I will not be afraid."

Fear may lead to anger and hostility, because those are ways by which people try to overcome fear. They strike out against the object that makes them afraid. The threat is not necessarily physical: Whatever makes another feel vulnerable can trigger a hostile response. Teachers must be alert to deal with causes rather than with effects.

Dealing with Emotions

Emotional responses become conditioned. The child who learns that anger brings a desired response will continue to meet that situation with anger. The child who finds that striking out at another person brings gratification will continue to do so. The child who once becomes fearful of an object or situation will continue to be fearful in that situation. Reconditioning is the process by which a tolerance is built up so that fear can be modified to the point where it is no longer threatening. The child who expresses frustration by anger will change only when such anger does not bring the desired result, when reward comes for asking, waiting, or taking one's turn.

In young children negative emotions tend to appear briefly, frequently, and intensely; they pass and the child is cheerful again. Children do not hold grudges. With their limited life experience, they may imagine a situation to be worse than it is, hence the intensity of their fear or anger. Only time can develop perspective. As they grow from child egotism to self-transcendence, they begin to realize that they are no more the center of people's hostility than they are of another's good will.

Children learn how to handle emotions positively when they are motivated to do so. If satisfaction comes by asking for something, and discomfort comes from taking it without permission, there is good reason to satisfy desires the pleasant way. They also learn from the example of people around them. In some households people say that they "enjoy a good fight." If that is the way people handle needs, children in such families bring the model to school and church. In families where people expect gentleness of one another, children are gentle wherever they are—unless experience indicates that their kindness encourages aggression in others. The contribution that a church school class makes to supplementing family patterns is the opportunity to talk about experiences with peers and to see the rationale for behavior.

The emotional development of children is important to church school teachers because the children bring their whole selves to the situation. Learning how to express emotions is part of religious development and education.

Sometimes teachers expect certain behaviors of children that they label *good.* They may even identify this with what it means to live as a Christian. The model is the quiet child who does not cause trouble and who answers questions, indicating knowledge of what the teacher has been trying to teach. But the Bible people whose stories we are teaching were not perfect. Let us be honest in teaching about the whole person. If you read the account from the Bible as well as the version in the teaching manual, you will have the whole story. The point of the Bible is that God uses people just as they are, fully human, and they are enabled by his grace to fulfill his purposes.

If teachers expect good conduct, they are saying something else by their actions: that only certain behaviors can make a child "good." To the small child the church, in a way, represents what God wants. This makes it important that a teacher's feelings toward specific actions do not interfere with warmth toward the whole child. Unacceptable behaviors present occasions for helping children understand the Golden Rule. These are opportunities of talking together, individually or as a group, about children's feelings toward

one another and toward adults. Children who seem to misbehave are not always in the wrong! They are sometimes misunderstood and unfairly treated, as they try to tell us.

We can help children deal with emotions by using biblical
material in which people show strong emotions. They are
used to seeing even violent outbursts on television programs.
Be honest in the use of story material from the patriarchal
families and their antagonisms. Children identify with Zacchaeus because he was a small person who had to climb a tree
in order to see. They identify with David because he beat up
the big fellow instead of becoming the victim. This emphasis
does not preclude understanding of the primary point. Zacchaeus found salvation when Jesus came to his house. David
felt confident that the Lord would deliver him because his
cause was just. These stories are not told primarily for emotional identification, but that is part of the interest they hold
for children.

The understanding of God is another way to help children
in their emotional growth. Think of all the ways in which the
Bible describes God: loving, tender, merciful, gentle, seeking, assuring; but also angry, judging, rebuking. Those who
did wrong broke the relationship with God. They suffered,
but God remained near, loving, waiting to restore the bond.
Recall the picture of Jesus in the gospels: calling people;
healing; speaking good news; and sometimes sharply criticiz-
ing those who wronged others, misinterpreted the word of
God, and caused injustice. It is not correct to identify gentleness with weakness, for only the strong dare be gentle. If
children are to understand the power of Jesus' identification
with the poor, hungry, dispossessed, and sinful—and know
that this is the calling of all Christians—they must understand his ability to show harshness and anger when he saw
God's children being neglected by those who had been called
to care about them.

Teachers Can Help

Another aspect of helping children lies in the way teachers handle their own emotions. Some teachers conceal their feelings, at times with difficulty. Children are sensitive to the moods of adults. They have to be, as adults are not always honest in disclosing how they feel. It is important for teachers to show that they, too, are human. Only God is perfect. So relax and be yourself! The children will feel more at ease. They are generous. They will forgive when you become impatient or angry. They know when they have been a cause of your feelings, but they need to know when they have done nothing to deserve your negative response. They need to know that adults, too, can feel fear. But in a threatening situation, children depend on the courage of adults to give them a sense of security.

Teachers can help children in a class situation to deal with their feelings in relationships with other children and teachers. This may take the form of intervention in specific situations. It could be the basis for discussion, built around a sharing of remembered experiences, a story, or a role-playing situation.

Richard M. Jones, a child psychologist, watched a group of children in a social studies class.[2] They were using advanced experimental material to learn how to think inductively. It was hoped that, by sharing in the experiences of the Netsilik Indians of northern Canada, depicted in color documentary films, they would understand how the lifestyle of a people is a result of their need to meet basic situations relating to food, shelter, and family. The emphasis was on cognitive learning. The children watched a caribou hunt, saw the red blood and the pitiful brown eyes of the creatures so unfairly matched as the men brought them to bay. Instead of appreciating the adaptive skills of the Eskimo (one of the course goals) they were viewing these people as unpleasant barbarians. A story was told about a grandmother, too weak to keep up with the rest of the tribe as they wandered across the winter's ice seeking shelter, who was gradually left behind to make her way alone in the cold. One discussion revolved around the situation of a family into which a baby girl had been born. If the family already·had more children than could be fed adequately, and no other family had adequate food so that they could adopt her, she would be left outdoors in the hope that another group of people might come by and rescue her.

The teacher who met with this group for dance and rhythm work the next period became aware that her class had become a place for providing release from emotional tension. During staff discussion, other teachers realized that they must go beyond the syllabus to help children express their response to these potentially frightening situations. They knew that hoped-for cognitive learning could be blocked by the intensity of emotional response. The sight of blood may arouse fear. Grandmothers are dearly loved. Babies are special. How could these things happen? The people who had so carefully constructed the unit of study with planned learning goals and lively teaching methods had neglected one important component: the children's emotional learning.

Much of the biblical material used in the church school has emotional content. Look at these stories not simply for religious content, or even moral content, but for the emotional content. Consider the situation of the baby Moses, young Samuel, and Isaac on his sacrificial journey. These are not stories written for young children, even though they are about children. If you find them in your teaching materials and decide to use them, be aware of where the child's identification will be. Emphasize the fact that Moses' mother, in preparing so carefully for putting the child by the river, including sending his sister to watch, was doing her best to save him. Admit that Samuel, who would have been about two years old when taken to Eli, might have been lonely for his parents. Suggest that Eli took good care of him, that Samuel (as the story affirms) was sure that God was near, and that he knew his mother would come to visit. If you ignore the child's feelings, you create a situation in which the child might wonder about God's love and care.

Children feel deeply and have not had the life experiences to help them explain their feelings. They do not understand their mixed feelings when a new baby comes to the family. They had looked forward to the new addition with expectancy; no one could have prepared them for the feeling of displacement. They knew that an infant would need special care. They did not grasp how long it would be before they had a playmate. As the months go by, the small child, helped by the rest of the family, sorts out feelings and can grow to accept the new member, realizing that there is always enough love for each person. The amazing discovery comes that there is no limit to love. It is never divided; it is shared.

Children and Death

Death also brings a variety of emotions. The young child never imagines death personally. Natural self-centeredness prevents this. A child may suffer loss, and any loss is a cause of grief. Because of the life span of many humans in our culture, even the death of a grandparent may be a rarity for young children. Yet there are accidents and death-dealing diseases. Children, like adults, experience grief as a mixture of emotions. They feel abandoned, and this can bring both fear and resentment. Could this happen to others they love? Could it happen to them?[3]

The religious response of adults is important. They are transmitting their own theological understandings. Some would say that God took the person, needed this person, or called the person to a higher (fuller, better) life. An explanation that may satisfy adults could make a child resentful of a God who took away someone loved, or fearful that God will act arbitrarily to take someone else. A child does not understand death as sleep, because people wake up, nor as eternal life, because that concept is beyond their comprehension. All that can be said confidently is that God loves people in life and death, that we are always in his love and care. Assure the child that God takes care of both the one who dies and those who continue to live. There is wisdom in those Christian traditions where people pray for those who have died, commending them as they enter God's eternal kingdom. This practice affirms that those who belong to Christ are united with him both in this life and in the world to come.

So it is for the child facing the possibility of death.[4] Humans usually find life good, despite its difficulties, and few rejoice at the prospect of death, even though they are taught that eternal life is a gift of God. The event of death is a crucial point in the life of every person, for the moment may be easy or difficult. Assurance is needed that one's life has been good and meaningful to others, that the love of those who are near surrounds and supports, and that their thoughts and prayer are near. Affirmation is given that the love of God strengthens, supports, and heals. The Christian's faith finds its assurance in the constant recollection of the resurrection. Jesus also passed through death into life. There is joy in this assurance. That is why the liturgical color for the Easter festival is white, and the color used for the funeral liturgy is also white. "He is not here, he is risen." "In Christ shall all be made alive."

CHAPTER 4

Aspects of

Learning

A L T H O U G H children learn in many ways, the most obvious way is through repetition. Parents and teachers believe that if one says to a child "Do this" or "Don't do that," the child will learn. But we are aware that other factors are involved. We know that the child must pay attention when directions are given. We know that repetition is important, but it is not clear how often it should be done, or what the spacing should be, and which works best as reinforcement.

Learning through repetition does not require much thinking; in fact, it may be impeded by the child who is always asking "Why?" or complaining "Do I have to do it again?" Boredom prevents learning.

Many of our actions are done as a matter of habit. It would be a waste of mental and emotional energy each day to think when to eat once it has been determined that a particular time is convenient for everyone involved. There is no reason to decide every Sunday morning whether or not to go to church. There is a rhythm to daily events that is comfortable and useful, freeing our minds for serious decision making. For a similar reason, teachers probably do not vary much the order of activities for each Sunday morning class session. Whatever value there might be in novelty would be cancelled out, because the children's preoccupation would be in shifting gears for the next new event. That is why the order of service for morning worship is not noticeably changed from week to week. Only on special occasions is there a difference, and this difference highlights the uniqueness of the event.

If forming habits is a useful simplification of daily life, it can also have drawbacks. One could get into a rut by doing the same things in the same way indefinitely, and change would then become difficult. The familiar is comfortable. When one feels secure, it seems unnecessary to change. Such an attitude stifles creativity. Routine living does not encourage problem solving, dreaming, projecting into the future, or any other process by which new perceptions might be formed.

Conditioning

Have you ever thought how habits are established or how they become changed? The process is called *conditioning*. The concept first came into prominence early in the century, when a Russian psychologist, Ivan Pavlov, found that when he rang a bell and then brought food to a dog, the dog began to salivate. Later, the dog would have the same response simply at the sound of the bell. An American psychologist,

John Watson, taught mice to run through a maze correctly by giving a mild electric shock whenever the mouse made a wrong turn. The animal learned how to avoid incorrect paths. Watson said that some children could be so carefully conditioned that they could be trained to become great musicians.

The most recent exponent of conditioning is B.F. Skinner.[1] He taught pigeons to perform specific tasks by releasing a pellet of food every time the birds made correct responses. He divided the tasks into simple units, each built upon the one previously learned. Out of this experiment Skinner developed some principles of learning.

Some people react negatively to the very mention of Skinner's name. They understand him as trying to reduce living to a set of mechanical responses. He may indeed believe that under carefully controlled circumstances learning can be accomplished through repetition and that people could live more free and creative lives through a carefully structured process of education. But his theories also describe ways people learn. Every parent or teacher has at some time wished that children could be trained to exhibit only "good" behavior. Then they add, "But children are only human, after all." We know that some acquired habits make life smoother for everyone in a family, classroom, or church. We know that an important technique for teaching is to start with a simple unit and move to one that is more complex. If you divide the Lord's Prayer into phrases, and write these on chalkboard or newsprint with a phrase on each line, six-year-old children will soon associate the correct words with the sounds they may earlier have memorized. They can begin to attach meanings to each phrase. Finally, they can put it together as a unit. You tell a story simply before filling in details.

Skinner's basic affirmation is that activity is the one way to characterize living beings. Humans are in a state of constant

activity. Education, therefore, must be a way of directing that activity toward agreed-upon goals.

People act in ways that bring a positive response. Since they need acceptance and approval, they tend to act in ways that will bring this (Skinner calls it positive reinforcement). They also act in order to avoid negative response, such as criticism, punishment, or loss of favor. This is called negative, or aversive, conditioning. In practical terms, children, as well as adults, do what succeeds and brings approval. If approval is given for *trying*, they will try even when they may not be able to succeed. If failure results in criticism, the child learns to give only safe responses. Such a child ceases to think, imagine, or try something new or difficult. The result is a limited amount of learning; no spontaneity, a loss of curiosity, inquiry, daring, and creativity. Sometimes teachers or parents do not put their feelings into words, but their manner or tone of voice indicates impatience or ridicule. You can encourage a child to develop in any direction by the response you give to his or her actions.

Consider classroom behavior. A child may be consistently disruptive, perhaps in a simple way like balancing a chair on one leg or surreptitiously hitting another child. This usually brings immediate attention from a teacher. Why do you think the child acts this way? One reason is to receive attention. The teacher has made this child successful when the behavior has brought the desired response. Even if the teacher speaks sharply or threatens dire consequences, the child's need has been fulfilled. The child who gets no attention from such tactics soon stops. Can one continue to let another child be annoyed? Of course not. The disruptive child is sent somewhere in the room where it is still possible to participate in activities but impossible to annoy someone else. The procedure must be followed every time the attention-getting device is used, until it stops. This is aversive conditioning, and it has usefulness in behavioral situations where other children need protection.

In cognitive situations (like giving an incorrect answer) positive conditioning is effective only if the response is to give the child a correct answer immediately in an encouraging way. The response is called feedback, and must be prompt and kind in order to be of positive reinforcement.

One can give positive reinforcement to the disruptive child by watching that child so carefully as to be able to give instant approval to each helpful action, by a word, a pat, or the request to do a special job "because you are being so helpful today." The child learns the message that helpful behavior works because it brings attention.

Teachers have used this technique patiently in special situations to teach a withdrawn child to speak, an unusually active child to sit quietly, or an anxious child to keep hands off other people. Such a technique does not get at the root of the problem causing the behavior, and there is thus a legitimate criticism of the technique. Yet the child can learn ways of acting in a class situation that give teachers more time in which to seek underlying causes of the behavior. Parents find that children at home also respond to such techniques.

Church school teachers are usually less concerned about the quiet child. They may even consider such a child to be good because the child is "no trouble," to use their phrase. Such a child may have problems, however. Why would a child be unwilling to join with others in tasks, or be seemingly unable to respond to other persons such as their teachers? Why would a child be unwilling to ask or answer a question? There could be fear, unwillingness to take risk, or a concern lest one be hurt. Life has taught some children that it is wise to say nothing, for then no one will criticize. Older children may have done this. Parents unthinkingly may have

However, the award system does not really serve the purpose of reinforcement, primarily because the reward is too long delayed. An expression of approval and of joy in work accomplished coming immediately upon the completion of a task or a correct response is a real reinforcement. Clearly, the rewards that cost nothing are more effective than those that cost money.

Teachers may be giving negative reinforcement. Some children have curious minds and are eager to explore. They want to learn about Bible people, trace the story of the church, or know how Christians are reaching out in many parts of the world. Meanwhile, we are busy trying to keep a large class minimally occupied or are concerned about interpersonal relationships and neglect developing the kinds of learning tasks these children need. Every such day in a Sunday school class gives negative reinforcement. As a result the child may protest at home against returning the next week. "We never do anything" is the complaint. Arrived in class despite protest, this same child may quietly withdraw, or else continue the protest by disruptive tactics in the class—remarks aimed at drawing laughter, or questions the child is certain the teacher cannot answer.

Programmed learning is a method that has been developed from Skinner's reinforcement theory. The learning machines used to give individualized basic instruction in reading and arithmetic skills, or subject knowledge in history or literature, are well-known, but programmed learning may also be found in book form. Some courses are available to teach biblical knowledge to young people and adults. The idea is to break down knowledge into small units, encourage correct answers, and permit the learner to advance at an individual pace.

The Learning Environment

Just as the reinforcement given to the learner is an important factor in learning, so also is the environment in which that learning takes place. The physical setting may invite or discourage learning. Children respond to light and color. Their curiosity is aroused by having many kinds of materials spread out for their use, to draw them into activity. They get the message that the session will be informal when the teacher invites them to sit on the carpeted floor or even, on occasion, to tumble around. They know that their special needs are being cared for when they can sit down to tables and chairs that are child-size.

Other rooms discourage learning. A small room that is used for a large class invites disruptive behavior by its crowdedness. If the teacher tries to compensate for the small room by conducting the class in a formal manner, with everyone seated around a table throughout the whole session, restlessness may result. When a few children are placed in a large room, the size is an invitation to use large muscles for running around and playing informal games. Chairs that are too small for older children, or too large for younger children, cause discomfort. This hardly encourages attention to other matters at hand. Walls bare of the visual aids that would catch the eyes of children are a monotonous sight. How different these are from the interest-provoking materials at elementary school: pictures, charts, samples of work accomplished, and questions for exploration! Children who gather during the week in this kind of physical environment may conclude that Sunday school is a dull place to be. What can anyone do without stimuli to learning? Teachers who care about children try to provide stimulating experiences. These need not involve expensive materials, but imagination is a necessary ingredient. There must be some equipment and material through which children can explore and learn.

People are the essential factor in the learning environment. Some have an easy, confident manner. They are sure of themselves and are constantly learning. Their whole approach is positive. Others are anxious lest they not teach well or fearful lest the children misbehave. They are probably better teachers than they realize, but they are not trusting themselves or the children. When teachers are working in a group with which they feel uncomfortable, they would be happier teaching another age group or doing some other job in the church.

The human environment is important to learning. Children affect each other's learning. Some, accustomed to using initiative at home and in school, work well with others, and everyone learns faster and better. They are generous and cooperative, thereby encouraging each other. Other children are aggressive. Unsure of themselves, they spend their time annoying others because that is the only way they can feel good. They need help.

The pastor is also involved in the learning process. Some clergy feel comfortable with children, quietly expressive or warmly expansive. Children are drawn toward such a person, gaily calling "Hi!" whether the meeting is on the street or in the church, sure of a warm response. The minister can come into the classroom as a resource person to explain biblical material, outline the church service, talk about the work of the church, or lead children on a tour of the church. Others seem forbidding to children, sometimes without realizing this. They may feel uncomfortable, wondering how to speak and act, fearful in advance that they will seem dull to children. Children quickly sense the feelings adults have about themselves and about children. They also are aware of genuine efforts people make to get acquainted. They do not like long presentations, which suggest that the speaker is afraid to stop talking lest someone ask an unanswerable question. Some clergy spend little time in the Sunday school. They say they have to be getting ready for or conducting the church service, or they are teaching an adult class. Other opportunities could be found for such visits. The adult class members could teach themselves occasionally (they are surely old enough to do this), or the minister could meet with the children after the church service, during vacation or weekday school, or at a family night program. No child should reach the age for church membership or confirmation class and only be getting acquainted with the pastor for the first time.

Another human factor in the learning environment is the whole "feeling tone" of the parish. Some churches seem impersonal, others are like one big family—and this feeling has nothing to do with size. This is especially evident on Sunday morning when the children are around. A church in which everyone feels welcome conditions the children (and newcomers) to feel that the church is a good place to be and that they are wanted. A church that ignores children, segregating them into Sunday school rooms, rarely making provision for them to be among adults, conditions them to feel unwanted. Think what it could mean to a child to be offered cookies and juice every Sunday morning while the adults have coffee hour. That is a continuous reward system. Whenever we want to express friendship, we invite people to eat with us. When this eating is done in company with people of all ages, the children are being told that they are an important part of the church.

Another factor is the way in which the church's provision for children compares with that of the community's schools. Where schools have both skilled, concerned teachers and up-to-date resources and learning opportunities, a church which has none of these will repel the child. There would

seem to be little positive to offer. When, however, the schools
are drab, lacking all stimulus, short on equipment, staffed by
teachers who long ago gave up hope of having any positive
response from children or encouraging assistance from ad-
ministration, then a church that provides loving and concerned teachers may become a positive stimulus. This is an
opportunity for creative religious education, but there would
be an enormous task of overcoming the negative feelings
children may have built up concerning the process of education. When both schools and churches have effective teachers and stimulating physical environments, the children live
in a situation where they can respond similarly in each situation. Sunday schools, meeting as they do only once a week,
are greatly helped in their efforts to provide creative learning experiences by the fact that newer methods and materials are familiar to the children who will use these easily on
Sunday.

Special Learning Needs

Fuller study could be made of the special learning needs
that some children have. Efforts have been made both in
materials for teaching and in research being carried on to
find effective methods for religious education. Blind children
have special needs for learning through the other senses.
Their presence can become an opportunity for sighted children to learn how to help people: when to offer assistance,
when to let the other try alone, what kinds of encouragement
are needed, and how to be sensitive to the other. Classes in
which a blind child is present would rely more on auditory
learning: stories, cassettes, records, experiences in action and
touch, and three-dimensional materials. Deaf children usually learn lip-reading at an early age. The class that includes
such a child will rely on visual materials and projects which

children construct individually or in small groups. They will encourage the child to speak and make the effort to understand sounds. Warm acceptance and friendliness is the keynote to the kind of environment the church can provide.

Emotionally disturbed children are usually full participants in school life. Teachers may think of them as disruptive (and occasionally withdrawn). (Remember that not every disruptive child has problems; some are simply bored with the session or anxious about something else at home or in school.) When untrained teachers deal with children who show strong hostility, they become bewildered when attempts to act reasonably are unrewarded. Some children are not able to cope with a Sunday session. There are too many children, and there is not enough individual help. If you know that a child in the class is in therapy, try having a helping teacher spend time with that child. This person may be your regular assistant or someone who relates easily to children and is willing to give a limited amount of time to help with a specific need. Keep a record from week to week of the child's activity during the session. It will be encouraging to look back after a few months and find some change. Some children are more content while sitting in the church service where less is demanded of them in interpersonal relationships. Others need a one-to-one relationship with a teacher.

This is a special ministry and you owe it to the parents as well as to the children, both of whom are members of the Christian community, to give them Christian nurture. You mediate the love of God by the very way in which you let the child know that some forms of behavior are acceptable and others are not. Some materials usually used in the curriculum may be threatening to children under emotional strain. Stories from the patriarchal families may remind them of their own jealousies. Other stories speak of abandonment or violence. Some experience-oriented stories arouse strong feel-

Parents are the first pesons who do such teaching, because they are with the child from infancy. As was pointed out earlier, the trust that an infant develops toward nurturing persons lays a groundwork for the kind of trust in God basic to religious faith on its deepest level.

Beginnings of Prayer

Prayer is a basic form of expressing our relationship to God. Through prayer, people express their needs for themselves and others, give praise and thanksgiving, and feel strengthened in their faith in God. Prayer is experienced in two settings: the personal prayer of the individual alone, at any place or time; and the prayer of the individual joined with that of others as a Christian congregation worships together. Each form of prayer is different, and each is essential for deepening the other. Those for whom prayer is essential to the spiritual life are eager that their children learn how to pray. It is important to realize that prayer both reflects and affects an understanding of God. Those who believe that God's love and justice are effective in every area of the life of persons and societies will express their personal needs and the wider concerns of others through prayer, believing that God's purposes will be accomplished. Those who believe that God has established a world that now functions under the natural laws inherent in the universe will see little reason for intercession. Parents and teachers need to consider deeply their personal understandings of God, because children are learning from them. The significance of family rituals, as well as forms of worship used in the Sunday school class, will come from the fact that understandings about God are being expressed through such rituals. Let us consider these observances.

By the time children are one year old, they are observing

family customs and imitating actions. Rituals for Sundays, holidays, meals, birthdays all take on meaning without verbal communication. As the child becomes two years old, the spoken words become understood. When there is a thanksgiving before meals, the child imitates the actions: head bowed, or hands clasped around the circle, standing or seated. When the Advent wreath is lighted or the figures are placed in the crèche, the toddler has a feeling of participation. Some have been taken into the church, heard the music, observed the rhythm of the service. In traditions that practice child baptism, some may have been old enough at the time of that event to have some awareness of what was happening, although most children who receive the rite do so in early infancy.

The three-year-old has developed a vocabulary. Many parents have taught the child an evening prayer by this time. As with other customs, they are sharing with the child an action meaningful to themselves. A child so young can have no understanding of what the word *God* means. When children even as old as eight or nine are asked how they think of God, they frequently picture an older person with a long beard— in spite of the fact that parents may have done nothing to foster such visualization. Is this transferred from Santa Claus? Have they heard Jesus called the Son of God and so pictured God from Sunday school pictures?

What the parent conveys about prayer to the three-year-old is an awareness of presence, an assurance of confidence and peace. Parents' words will be more helpful than most of the rhymed verse that goes by the name of children's prayers. The child's own words at least express a three-year-old's understanding. Share these moments. Say "For what shall we say 'thank you' to God?" Children like to follow the phrases aloud. The idea of silent or interior prayer has little meaning.

Remember that the child is forming an understanding of

God through this experience. The words spoken should convey the idea that God is one who gives, who is good, loving, and trustworthy. God also provides the environment in which the child lives: world, family, and friends. God understands hurts, fears, angers; is comfortingly near in the darkness as well as in the brightness of the morning. Some parents have been known to convey understandings of God as one who punishes and should be feared, who makes strict rules that must not be disobeyed. Such ideas do not belong to the past. The all-seeing God who looks for wrongdoing rather than good is another expression of Santa Claus, who might leave lumps of coal in the Christmas stocking instead of gifts. As small children are sensitive to the feelings of adults, this idea could be conveyed by someone who says lovingly but reprovingly, "God loves you and is very sorry when you do something like this." Adults who withhold love from the erring child in the misunderstanding that this is "light" punishment may make a child fearful of total abandonment. Nevertheless, all adults will be misunderstood by children at some time; usually, this is self-correcting. No one is completely consistent.

People who live around children convey their religious understandings most clearly by the way they meet life. When children see that adults feel assured of help when they are in trouble or respond in joyous thanksgiving in times of happiness, something deeply and truly religious becomes understandable.

Learning in Church

By the age of three years, many children are already in contact with a church. They have been taken to nursery class. Another person, the teacher, begins to tell them about God. In company with other children they experience expression of prayer. They learn that other people also address God, and that this can be a group experience. They learn other dimensions to the knowledge of God. They learn to sing simple songs of praise and hear verses of scripture. This takes them beyond the familiar Christmas carols and the Christmas story. Few Bible stories convey religious meaning to children at this age; most would be more confusing than enlightening. These children must learn of God through experience, and biblical verses may better affirm this experience. They have heard about Jesus at Christmas time. They may even think of him only as a baby. This is why the nursery class tries to introduce some simple stories about Jesus and his loving outreach toward people.

The child knows from experience the meaning of doing wrong, the feeling of alienation, the struggle to seek forgiveness, and the joy of restoration. Children also know about anger, although they may not know why they feel this way. They feel hostility but cannot conceptualize the causes. Moralizing will not help, nor will telling them to be like Jesus. Problems in human relationships should be dealt with on a personal level. Leave alone the child's growing relationship with God; love is tender and develops slowly. At its beginnings, it should not be complicated by negative responses.

The preschool child acts and feels; this is why that age is referred to as the sensorimotor stage. Good feelings come from doing what adults expect because they respond pleasantly. But it is not possible to please anyone all the time. Adult demands, and even those of peers, can become overwhelming. Share with the child moments of gladness: thanksgiving for the warmth of love, the joy of reconciliation, the pleasure of sharing and doing for another, the beauty of the world. Share moments of comfort and security in being found when one is lost, feeling better when one has been ill, becoming quiet after anger, or having rest when one is tired.

Participation in family rituals takes on more meaning as the child grows and has more means of communication. The child of three or older can say a prayer of thanksgiving, sing Christmas carols, and follow the actions of the church service. Children feel themselves to be part of the church's fellowship as opportunities are made for them to participate.

The kindergarten child continues to increase in verbal ability, learning to interact with others, use graphic materials, retell stories, and repeat songs. More materials can be used than were possible with the three-year-old, but it is unwise to try to include more difficult biblical stories. The child's verbal ability should not be overestimated; remember that it has little connection with conceptual understanding. The Bible stories you think childlike may actually confuse the child who is developing an understanding of God's love. Teachers enjoy four- and five-year-olds because they are responsive. But satisfying as it may be to a teacher's or parent's ego, do not give deeper meaning to their religious questions than is warranted. They think concretely; and theology is an abstract subject.

Elementary Children

Six- to ten-year-olds are in a different category. Whether one calls this the age of industry (Erikson) or the concrete-operational age (Piaget), a similar picture comes to mind. These children have questing minds, curiosity, imagination, a desire to work and to achieve, and some skills for coping with difficulties and disappointments. Before generalizing about their religious development, let us look at some of the religious research.

Ronald Goldman, a well established religious educator in England and Australia, showed children a picture of a child kneeling beside a bed. The child in the picture was identified as someone of their own age praying alone. The purpose of using the picture was to elicit the understanding of God held by children at varying ages. Children were asked specific questions such as the following in response to the picture: "Most people have a picture or an idea of God (Jesus, Spirit) in their minds when they pray. What is the picture or idea of God (Jesus, Spirit) this child has when praying?"[1] It will not come as a surprise to many to learn that six-year-olds see God in physical terms; here are some replies: "A nice person who will like you." "He has a cloak and long hair, a beard and short trousers." "He'd look pretty and his face'd look old." God is "up there" or "up in the sky." Several said that he would look like Jesus. Between the ages of ten and twelve, the superhuman aspects are noted. "He'd be standing in the clouds with lots of glory around." Not until the age of fourteen does a child say "You can't describe God because he can't be seen."

David Elkind, a child psychologist well-versed in the psychology of Piaget, has studied children's understandings of prayer. By asking children questions in an open-ended manner, he encourages them to probe meanings.[1] He found that five- to-seven-year-olds have a vague notion of prayer as somehow linked with God. They see it as being engaged in at fixed times, such as bedtime or meals. Seven- to nine-year-olds see prayer in terms of particular activities. It is concrete, answering personal needs and desires. The nine- to twelve-year-olds understand prayer as conversation with God. What one thinks is more important than what one says. They can internalize prayer. They know that not everyone prays. They understand the meaning of thanksgiving and intercession. They know that they pray in a time of need, and they understand when there seems to be no answer. Prayer is satisfying; it is connected in their minds with pleasant emotions.[2]

Parallel to this development from concrete to more abstract thinking is the child's understanding of holidays.[3] Younger children think of Christmas and Easter in terms of what they receive, such as Christmas gifts or Easter candy. Older children are just beginning to grasp the significance of these celebrations in the Christian church. "It is when Jesus was born"; "It has something to do with the resurrection," they will say.

Elkind's conclusions are that going through developmental stages is natural, and children can be expected to come out eventually with normative interpretations, whatever misconceptions they may entertain in early childhood. He assumes, as a practical matter, that children will be exposed to religious experiences before they are ready to assimilate meaning, but they give up earlier explanations as their reasoning ability develops. The processes of accommodation and assimilation are going on as the child accommodates the abstract to the concrete, and assimilates more mature understandings of prayer to the childlike ones that served earlier needs. Elkind concludes, "The child can experience religious emotion before he can entertain religious thoughts. He must be shown."[4] He adds that children are like adults more in feelings than in concepts. It is important that children at an early age participate in church rituals and the celebration of religious holidays with their families.

Understanding Faith

In other words, children apprehend more than they comprehend. Their understanding develops slowly from experience. Unlike Goldman, Elkind does not feel that incorrect understanding becomes fixed and will later have a negative effect on the child's response to the Christian faith. Rather, early notions are outgrown, dropped, or reformulated into more mature patterns of thought. However children interpreted religious "truth" was appropriate for that particular age; reinterpretation on a conceptual level is a task for a later age. One cannot wait to tell children about God, teach them how to pray, or take them to church services. They will learn about some of these activities from the community if parents do not initiate the experience. This does not mean that teachers should use material before there can be concrete understanding, but that some of the religious tradition will be interpreted by the child in stages. Inevitably, information is picked up simply because a child belongs to a religious family and participates in the life of a church. Religion is also observable through interaction with neighborhood children.

Younger children who ask abstract ethical or doctrinal questions are not looking for the abstract answers older children might need.[5] Their *why* questions are concrete, as Piaget pointed out. This means that some material may be easily learned, and even memorized, but not understood. A teacher needs to decide what material is important enough to be learned before it can be cognitively understood.

The age of six, when the child begins to become aware of human limitations and to get beyond the idea of magic, is important in the development of the understanding of God. The young child has thought of the parent as all-powerful, and this is comforting when he or she experiences feelings of helplessness. By the age of six, however, children have learned through experience that parents are not all-powerful. They are human and limited. This time of life becomes important in the development of the understanding of God.[6] Here is one who is indeed dependable and trustworthy. Any identification of parent and God, in either direction, is broken. The child becomes less egocentric and more able to seek ends beyond the personal. This makes it possible to understand that God cares for others as well as to pray for others.

The Christian child is early introduced to stories about

Jesus. Both the words and intonations used suggest theological elements. The child understands the humanness of Jesus —an essential element in Christian understanding. Bible stories convey the picture of someone loving and concerned to help. Older children are ready to understand the sense of conflict, the opposition to Jesus, his own harsh criticism of some of the leaders and their actions. If the gospel meaning is to be conveyed, the teacher will read verses that give the reaction of those who saw and heard him: "They marvelled at his teaching"; "They said, 'who is this?' " He aroused a sense of wonder. When the teacher's own sense of commitment is deep, this reverence is conveyed through verse and story. Telling the child, as a theological principle, that Jesus was divine, or God's Son, may express only an intellectual conviction. The mystery of his being is more subtly conveyed. This is how to begin understanding the Christian confession, "Jesus is Lord." Since God is the Lord, this word is applied to Jesus because his actions convey the meaning. This sense of wonder breathes through the birth narratives, with angel choir and wise men from the East. It is expressed through the feelings of the crowds pressing upon him, responding to his touch, rejoicing in his presence. It is clear in the resurrection narratives, wherein he appears and withdraws, recognition coming suddenly to those who saw him. There was something different, yet at the same time familiar, about this figure. Peter, in the fishing boat exclaimed, "It is the Lord"; the two disciples at Emmaus said to each other, "Did not our hearts burn within us?"

The Christian understands God as trinity: creator, redeemer, and sanctifier—the one who makes holy. This may be considered an intellectual definition of the understanding of God. It could also be interpreted as a description of the aspects of God. From this living awareness of how God acts, Christians are able to confess the historic creeds—not as definitions but as descriptions. The child may find it difficult to understand Holy Spirit as God working through persons, church, and world. The word *spirit* reminds them of Hallowe'en ghosts. Spirit is best explained in other terms, such as a happy spirit, or the spirit of a place, phrases that say that the word speaks of life. The child begins to be aware that God is known in several ways: as the creator to whom they can turn in every need; like Jesus, loving, healing, and reconciling; like the Spirit, making it possible for each person to grow in love and joy.

When a child becomes older and is able to conceptualize will be the time to put this understanding into some recognizable theological form. Then analogies and symbols may be useful. After the child has experienced God in many ways, he or she will be ready to pull the threads together and know what is meant by the idea of trinity.

Faith and Relationships

The child's understanding of God develops not only through biblical stories and prayer but through lived relationships. Do not expect adult ethical understandings in children of elementary school age. Remember that children take a literal view of justice. Simply act lovingly and justly and expect children to grow in understanding. Their sense of justice is good. "Getting away with something" makes the world seem unstable. To know what is right and what is wrong gives a feeling of security. Keep this in the perspective of personal relationships. Help the child decide what is right to do for a person in a particular situation rather than absolutize right and wrong.

There are school situations that cause anxiety. The learning of basic skills may challenge curiosity and give a sense of achievement, but it also may be a source of strain. If we try reading nonsense syllables, we will have some idea of what it means for a child to learn how to read. Words make little sense at first, and it takes time to get them sorted. The assurance that God loves and cares, whether one succeeds or not, is important to the child's sense of self-worth. Acceptance by parents and teachers is also needed. Too many people connect their self-image with achievements and successes. That is unfortunate, because failure is one element in human experience. Good learning can take place through mistakes and failures. A child's faith can become a source of strength in times of anxiety.

There are continuing experiences with peers that can arouse both fear and hostility. It is impossible to like everyone all the time. It is impossible to have one's own way all the time. Rejection is as difficult for children as for adults. Learning how to get along with others is a long process, and there will be hurts. The child needs to be assured of God's love, even when friends shut one out.

There are also needs at home. How misunderstood a child can feel sometimes! Brothers and sisters seem unfair. Parents seem to have favorites. Getting along in a family is not easy. Because family members can trust one another's love, they seem to feel more free to express real feelings, although sometimes with devastating effect. How can children be helped to know that anger masks fear as well as hostility, that people can love but act unlovingly? They usually sense this. They are forgiving as well as resigned to the ways adults act; with brothers and sisters it is more difficult. Religion is not an escape. It is a way of experiencing forgiveness, learning how to be forgiving, and understanding the meaning of reconciliation.

Preadolescents

When children reach the age of about eleven, religious maturity begins to show. They can think abstractly and understand in ways unknown to younger children. They begin to have a sense of history and a feeling for the future, which makes it possible for them to delay demands and to know that situations change.

They begin to understand the meaning of commitment. It would not be fair to say that an adolescent's or adult's commitment is stronger than that of a child's. All commitments are in need of renewal, because no one is completely faithful in keeping promises. In many Christian traditions it is customary for older boys and girls to be invited to make their commitment to Christ. Such a commitment presupposes an understanding of who Christ is and what he means in terms of their life. Commitment to Christ was never meant to be a logical contract by which a person promises to do certain things. Rather, the practice grows out of the commitment, and the latter is a response in love, trust, and faith. A person commits the whole self. How old need one be in order to love others? What a ridiculous question! But the Christian church asks for evidences of commitment in terms of life. Those evidences will take certain forms for older boys and girls, but their deepest response may come much later.

This is where religious development is leading: to the fullness of the Christian life.

CHAPTER 6

Growing

into Moral

Persons

P A R E N T S and teachers desire children to grow into moral persons. Although this is an important goal for families and churches, no one has ever discovered any way of guaranteeing such a result. Sometimes people are so concerned about *how* to do this that they have not clearly thought about *what,* specifically, they wish to accomplish.

What is morality? Or, in other words, what does it mean to act as a moral person? A parent will say "Hang up your coat.

That's a good boy." A teacher will say, "Put your books in the desk drawer. Good!" But children who are called good because they are neat are not necessarily morally good. They have kept the rules and obeyed the authorities. In this sense, to throw the coat on the floor or leave the books on top of the desk is "bad" or "wrong." To give obedience the same emphasis that one gives in granting approval to sharing toys or channeling anger is to base morality on doing what someone else says is right. It does not lead to autonomy in making moral decisions.

Preparatory to growth as moral persons is an understanding of the distinction between rules and principles. The rule is concrete. The Ten Commandments, for example, are in this category. Rules are important because they set boundaries. Principles by which lives are guided are broader. They are related to how we treat other persons. The Golden Rule is in this category; so is Leviticus 19:17, "You shall love your neighbor as yourself." It does not tell a person specific ways through which to show love to one's neighbor. It supposes an understanding of what is meant by loving the self. One could make up rules that spell out a meaning for loving one's neighbor, but the statement was not intended that way. As it stands, personal decisions are required. Loving one's neighbor might indicate one form of behavior in a given situation and another in a different context.

Even when the intent of a rule is clear, personal interpretations and decisions may have to be made. "You shall not steal" is the command (rule), but in Victor Hugo's classic story *Les Miserables,* the man who stole in order to buy bread for his starving family was forgiven. He had done wrong, but the implication is that under certain situations of stress wrongdoing can be condoned. The parallel situation is the much-used "Heinz" dilemma of Harvard psychologist Lawrence Kohlberg, in which a man steals expensive medicine he could not afford to buy in the hope of saving his wife's life.

Fifty years ago a team of researchers at Yale University under the heading "Studies in Deceit" came up with the finding that, although honesty is a much-taught virtue, everybody is deliberately dishonest in some way at some times. One cannot teach morality in the abstract, although one may talk about it. It is taught and learned in the concreteness of everyday life. How to make ethical decisions is basic for education in morality.

Methods

There are several ways through which people have tried to train children in moral living. The one begun earliest is conditioning. The child who obeys is rewarded. Disobedience brings punishment. When the command is in the area of moral values, parents and teachers hope that they are assisting the child to internalize right responses. The most obvious example is the discipline in classroom or home. Hitting another child is not tolerated. Various forms of negative conditioning are used, such as separating the child, taking away privileges, or explaining why this is unacceptable behavior. Showing kindness wins a positive response, such as words of approval or a special favor. The simplest, quickest method is usually the most effective. That conditioning can effectively train people to make moral choices is an assertion that thoroughgoing behaviorists will make but others doubt. Some children have been so well conditioned to tell the truth that a guilty look reveals any evasive answer. The lie-detector test is based on this kind of conditioning. Changes in heartbeat and breathing are assumed to be indicators of guilt feelings; a person so conditioned could never be trusted to head off pursuers in search of a companion. However, such a method does not enable people to develop the ability to make ethical decisions.

A second method is that of modeling. Parents and teachers become examples of the moral person. If such a person is a rule keeper, the child will seek approval by conscientiously trying to keep all rules. Following parental models is so subtle and pervasive that this dimension of education has never been fully explored. Teacher models are less effective because their time with children is limited, so it can be assumed that basic moral behavior is learned at home. Parents who go beyond rule keeping—open, generous people who trust others and are sensitive to the needs of others—are models for another kind of moral development. Their children will grow up trusting other people.

Still a third method is that of moral reasoning. It is an approach that assumes human beings can think about behavior and act accordingly. Much emphasis is being laid on this approach today and much of the following discussion will delineate it.

Developmental Theories

Reference has been made earlier to developmental approaches in childhood education. These have implications for moral development. Erikson builds on Freudian theory to outline distinctive stages as he sees them. The ability to trust, gained or not gained during the first two years of life, is a factor in the growth of a person who can feel free to be forgiving, generous, and committed to other people and causes. The struggle of wills in the two- and three-year-old leads to the internalization of *no* and *yes* with reference to the role of the parent as authority figure. Erikson and Freud lay particular stress on ages four and five, the Oedipal stage, when they see children developing identifications with the parent of the same sex. In so doing, these children internalize the will of the parent as conscience. (Freud's term is *superego*.) Parental will is equivalent to the divine will. The later discovery that parents are not perfect comes as a troublesome but eventually accepted fact. During school years, the morality of school and peer group plays a role in development. Where Freud stressed the war between ego and id within the personality, Erikson was more impressed by the unity achieved within the ego. He stressed ego-identity as a task of adolescence and saw the importance of ego strength as a basis for ethical action. Human freedom involves the ability to make choices.

Piaget, the basic exponent of structural development, based his theory of morality on the assertion that children act in specific ways because of the stage of cognitive development they have reached. They can be trained to act in certain ways, but the reasons they give for their actions indicate their stage of moral development. Piaget observed this process while watching children play marbles. The youngest shot marbles at random; those aged four to six tried to play the game. The oldest were conscious of the rules as a fact of social behavior. Younger children thought rules were immutable; older children felt free to modify rules to suit the situation. Recall Piaget's example of the children who broke the cups. To the younger children, the damage done determined the punishment. Older children, able to reason about principles, placed intention first. As children grew older, they were able to distinguish between mistaken statements, "white lies," and deliberate attempts to mislead. If Piaget is correct, it requires a certain level of cognitive development to become a fully moral person.

Kohlberg sought to authenticate the validity of such categories of moral thinking through a series of "dilemmas" offered for solutions to seventy-five boys between the ages of

10 and 16 from middle- and working-class backgrounds living in the Chicago area. He continued his surveys as the boys grew older in order to see if and how their thinking changed, and found a development in moral thinking. It is important to note here that Kohlberg was talking about moral *thinking,* not moral *acting.* He wanted to uncover the processes through which people make moral decisions, and he did this by finding out why they thought one solution to the dilemma was better than another. This does not say that, under the stress of an immediate situation, one would act in accordance with one's cognitive ability to grasp a moral solution. But given the factor of development, sixteen-year-olds will probably act differently from six-year-olds; at least they will give different reasons for their actions.

Kohlberg's Theory

Like Piaget, Kohlberg speaks of levels and affirms that people pass from one level to another. He subdivides each level into two stages.[1] Holding to developmental theory, he says that a person in one stage will sometimes act in accordance with a lower stage of thinking and sometimes begin to act as if in the next stage. There is no timetable as to how long one will remain in a stage, but no one ever skips a stage. Most people never go beyond the fourth stage. It satisfies their image of how to act as a moral person. Some reach stage five, and a few reach stage six.

Younger children, grades one to six, are in level one, pre-conventional morality. They are trying to keep the rules. They understand specific meanings for good and bad, right and wrong, with reference to how authority figures define the terms. There are two stages to this level. In stage one, ages six and seven, obedience is given to the rules in order to escape punishment. There is no concern for moral order or the rightness of the authority. The object, quite simply, is to avoid pain. In stage two, ages eight and nine, the child does right in order to satisfy needs. This may include satisfying the needs of others in what may seem like reciprocity but is really done in order to be accepted, rewarded, or in some other way satisfied. Loyalty and personal relationship do not enter the transaction.

Older children may be entering level two, the conventional level, comprised of stages three and four. Such persons are developing a feeling of loyalty to the group—family, school, peer group, or community—and a sense of identity within the group. In the third stage, which Kohlberg calls the good boy-nice girl orientation, the child of about ten acts in ways that will win approval. Lest this seem to be the same as stage two, one can understand the progress in terms of intention: In stage two the child was concerned only with personal need satisfaction; in stage three part of the personal satisfaction comes from incorporation into group goals. Children here are less egocentric and are developing the ability for wider relationships. Their selfhood is not threatened by being part of a social group. Stage four is referred to as the law and order orientation. Right behavior consists in keeping the law, respecting authority, and helping to maintain the social order. Most people would say that this is a commendable way to act; most legal systems are oriented in this direction.

The third level (stages five and six) is the postconventional, also referred to as the autonomous or principled, level. To be autonomous is to be oneself, to have a fully formed ego, and to be able to make decisions without undue reference to consequences, such as whether there will be reward or punishment, whether one is approved or has a feeling of contributing to group maintenance. This level, says Kohlberg, is only possible when people have attained sufficient cognitive development to make reasoned decisions. It could not be expected before adolescence. Stage five is a social contract orientation. It goes beyond the law-and-order stage, because one acts in certain ways in order to serve the highest social good. A person at this stage would not be obedient to any law simply because it is law, but might work to change existing laws in the interest of the common good. This leaves place for conscientious objection; in American parlance, the higher law. Stage six, seldom attained according to Kohlberg, is that of universal ethical principle. This presupposes that the fully moral person will have an informed conscience that sets rules that will benefit the most people. These are abstract, ethical principles like the Golden Rule. They embody universal principles of justice and respect for individuals.

While the last level is not of primary concern to teachers of children, if this is the ultimate goal of moral development, the intent should be understood. Kohlberg has presented his dilemmas to children in non-Western cultures and finds a similarity in their stage development. He affirms that moral reasoning is not a transmissive process but a restructuring of experience through the interaction between the child's cognitive structure and that of the environment. Kohlberg also insists that to say one level is higher than another gives a goal for attainment, but it is not meant to be a basis for judging people whose lives are satisfactory at another stage. The value of a person does not depend on that person's being in a particular stage. Each succeeding stage is simply a better *way* of acting.

However, critics affirm that there is a philosophical viewpoint in the stages and a definite understanding of what constitutes justice and what principles are most moral.[1] It is asserted that IQ, sophistication, and education produce higher "scores" in response to answers given to the solution of the dilemmas. Theoretically, basic structural, and therefore invariant, concepts emerge in answers given to any content (that is, the dilemmas, which are hypothetical story situations), but in practice, educational factors seem to affect answers. These same critics state that there is no reason to assert that a morality of universal social forms is higher than a morality of social contract or of law and order. If one accepts stages in moral development, it is important first to understand the philosophical assumptions out of which each grows, to know what the researcher means, and whether a particular person or institution (parent, teacher, school, or church) accepts these goals.

Aspects of Moral Education

Robert H. Havighurst (who earlier wrote on developmental stages) and Robert F. Peck studied character development in adolescents in a small midwestern city in the 1950s.[2] They identified five character "types" through which people might move, all of which could be found among adolescents and adults, but indicated that most people stay at the second type. The five types are: the amoral during infancy; the expedient beginning in early childhood; the conforming (doing the expected) and the irrational–conscientious (following one's internal standard) in later childhood; and the rational–altruistic (objectively assessing an act in a given situation) rarely achieved by adolescents. They observed three characteristics concerned with the perception of other people that seemed to affect development. These were: observation—accuracy of perception of how people behave; insight—accuracy of recognition of what other people want and how they feel; empathy—degree of ability to feel with others' emotions, aims, and behavior from their point of view.

In any discussion of moral education three aspects are being considered; reasoning, judgment, and behavior. While one must recognize these three elements in an ethical situation, the decision made is based also on nonrational factors.[3] The area of empathy and involvement, even vicariously, enters into moral decision-making. Children learn how to develop moral judgment, even perhaps how to act morally, as they first learn how to enter empathetically into a given situation. Empathy is developed through the methods of teaching used.[4] Assuming that narrative and anecdote (for example, the dilemma or case-study technique) is a basic form, this may be presented in several ways. Story telling is a skill. The tone of voice tells hearers with whom to identify. Role-playing is an important technique. By taking different roles, children become aware of the many dimensions of a situation. Films, especially brief ones, are an excellent means of becoming immersed in a situation; so is a television program. The use of simulation games causes players to invest much of themselves with the desire to win and anxiety about losing. Games such as Monopoly may be played simply to win in the abstract, but they can also reveal ethical attitudes by the way players handle the impetus to win. Each method needs to be followed by discussion to clarify the content of the situation, help participants explore their feelings, reflect, enunciate the principles they have learned, and make decisions.

Moral Development in Christian Perspective

Is there any difference between moral judgment as the schools wish to develop this and the church's perspective? Values clarification has become a widely used method of helping people assess how strongly they hold specific moral precepts. They may be asked to rank a number of objects in order to determine what things are really essential to everyday life. They may be given statements on a continuum to decide how much or how little they agree. These techniques, as developed by Sidney Simon and Louis Raths, are outlined in books designed for use in teaching.[5] Their usefulness lies in doing exactly what the name *values clarification* suggests: helping individuals clarify what is valuable to them. Within what limits are they willing to live for certain principles? How far would they go in helping another person ("Do unto others . . .")? How much would they give up for ecological reasons or to feed the hungry? Which hungry people concern them—their own families, neighbors, or people 10,000 miles away? Clarification brings insights. One finds it necessary to define a philosophy and admit to oneself how strongly one really holds a principle when it comes to actions that might be uncomfortable to oneself. Values clarification does not tell anyone what is right or wrong. That is not its purpose, although teachers who use these techniques can proceed into that area if they so desire. People who affirm that each situation determines the ethical way to teach would supplement the exercises by discussing the reason for each decision.

Values clarification can deal with real situations. For example, a group of young people were asked to rank the value of using seatbelts. Then each was asked how often he or she had used seatbelts during the past week and month. There was no necessary correlation between the principle and the practice. Some who believed absolutely in the need to have seatbelts seldom remembered to use them. The process of clarifying values helped these young people see the gap between what they affirmed (seatbelts are necessary for safety) and what they practiced (most did not use seatbelts regularly). Essentially, the values clarification process is nonjudgmental. It is not critical of how a person acts. The reasoning here is that to make judgments would adversely affect a person's willingness to give honest answers. People would give the answer they thought was expected. Everyone who teaches religious education classes knows how easily this happens even in less sensitive areas.

Any person who values other humans will try to act in ways that assist in their well-being. One does not have to be religious in order to be good. What then is distinctive about a Christian approach to moral development? Basically, it lies in the reason for an action and the dynamic by which one lives. The Christian acts in love and justice as a response to God who made us, loves us, and commands his people to show love and justice to others as evidence of their calling. Obedience to his command is an expression of this relationship.[6] Kohlberg's use of the Golden Rule in stage six thinking is instructive. He would seem to imply that at this stage religious orientation would be a factor in moral judgment. This statement of Jesus was also a teaching of the rabbis, and it is found in other religious traditions. One cannot abstract such a sentence without reference to the context of law and covenant in which it was spoken. The chosen people were expected to be faithful. When Christians quote the two so-called great commandments (Deut. 6:5 and Lev. 19:18)—to love God and one's neighbor—the vertical dimension of relationship to God is inextricably bound into the horizontal dimension of human relationships.

The Christian could not affirm, with level five thinking, that the social contract is an ultimate form of morality. Society was responsible for the crucifixion of Jesus. Society persecuted the church for three centuries. It is possible for the minority to be right. God, not social contract, is the lawgiver. However, the recognition of the role of the community in level five is more biblical than the highly personal decision making of level six. Biblical writers insist that people must live morally as an expression of their membership in a community under a God who is just—whether these be the people of Israel or those in the first Christian congregations. The community of Israel accepted Torah at Sinai and reaffirmed it during the reign of King Josiah and upon the return from Babylonian exile under Ezra and Nehemiah. The Christian community wrote and preserved the gospels and epistles in which their laws are affirmed. What differentiates this from stage four thinking seems to be the emphasis in the latter on maintaining a given social order, whereas the Christian community maintains the freedom to change.

The levels of development about which the Christian parent and teacher are concerned have to do with the child's growing awareness of the presence of God in the world and in individual lives. They strive to develop a sense of love and trust that is without fear, and an empathy with the needs of others that makes possible acts of generosity and self-giving. They hope for a commitment to Christ, whose life, death, and resurrection are the prototype of the transforming power of God.

CHAPTER 7

A Child's

Commitment

CHRISTIANS have long pondered what commitment to Christ can mean for children. New Testament records describe the conversion of adults, from other forms of religion, who responded to a call to repentance and affirmed that they believed in Jesus Christ as Lord. They were baptized and received the gift of the Holy Spirit, although there is one narrative in which the gift preceded baptism. At least one family is known to have been converted: that of the jailor at Philippi, where the apostle Paul had been imprisoned. Since the ages of the family members are not known, the baptism of children can be neither proved nor disproved by this event.

Early Practice

Adult baptism was the norm for the first few centuries after Christ. Indeed, many adults, including the Emperor Constantine, delayed baptism until they were near death, believing that to sin after baptism was more serious than before the act. The great theologian Augustine, writing in the fourth century, set out the idea that, because all are born with original sin, stemming from Adam, it is necessary for infants to be baptized immediately, lest they die in sin. (The idea of original sin, however interpreted, is a Christian exegesis of Genesis 2). Paul interprets this as the reason for the death and resurrection of Christ: the event that necessitated a new relationship to be established between God and creation. Eventually, infant baptism became the norm for a thousand years. The question was also raised as to when a child would be able to sin. The consensus among theologians was that the first six years were a time of innocence, and beyond that time a child's reasoning powers made it possible to recognize when actions were wrong and obedience to God and parents deliberately violated. The need for an act of repentance, incorporated into the office of penance as preparation for receiving the sacrament of Communion, developed subsequently.

The Reformation did not initially change this understanding. However, one group of Protestants who wanted a more radical reform than that provided by Luther, Calvin, and the English church, became known as Anabaptists, in part because they insisted on the necessity of rebaptism (*anabaptism* means *another baptism*) for adults who had been baptized as infants. They insisted that only adults could make a confession of faith in Christ and only at that point should persons be baptized. They left unanswered the question of the effects of original sin for the eternal salvation of children.

Devout Puritans had their own answer. Their method of child rearing was to break the will of the young as soon as possible after infancy. This was done lovingly but insistently so that children trusted their parents completely and gave unquestioning obedience. This docility was tested in late adolescence when young men "sowed their wild oats." The remembrance of the past aroused feelings of guilt that led to a sense of sin, repentance, and the transfer of unquestioning trust and obedience to God. This was their experience of being born again.[1]

Methodist child-rearing practice in the late eighteenth and early nineteenth centuries strove for the conversion experience at an early age. When one realizes the high child mortality rate at that time in England and the United States, it is understandable that parents who feared the flames of hell for the unrepentant would seek means of bringing young children to face the reality of sin in their lives. Children's story books recounted the deaths of children who witnessed to the joy of their salvation and warned readers to be vigilant.[2] Children were instilled with an acute awareness of guilt, a sense of sin, and a fear of damnation, in order that they might come to the joyous relief of forgiveness, divine acceptance, and belief that their reward would be in heaven.

Horace Bushnell, a Connecticut Congregational minister (1802–1876), protested this form of evangelism through fear, though he acknowledged the need for personal decision. It did not seem sensible to him that children brought up in a home with loving parents practicing their Christian faith could ever feel so sinful as to believe God would reject them unless they repented with feelings of guilt and fear. On the contrary, children growing up in a Christian atmosphere would feel assured of God's love.[3] Some interpreters of Bushnell's book *Christian Nurture* developed the idea that a conversion experience was not necessary to commitment. The decision to follow Christ could be made at any age and might not be discernible through a dramatic experience. This form of faith is illustrated in Philip Greven's study of the Protestant temperament by the group he calls the moderates, people who tried to live and practice the Christian faith in their daily lives through families, work, and churches, but for whom emotional experiences were not a part of religious development.[4]

Stages in Faith

Consider the child who grows up within the religious framework of a church-related family. The parents view this child as a gift from God to be received thankfully as a trust. Churches that practice believers' (adult) baptism frequently provide a service of dedication through which child and congregation can give thanks for the new life, and the child be received into the congregation through the family. This child is not technically a Christian, because no personal commitment of faith has been made.

Those traditions that practice infant baptism have a different kind of presentation. Whether the infant is immersed (as in the Eastern Orthodox tradition), sprinkled, or has water poured on the head, this is the rite of baptism. It is done in faith that God has acted, his grace has been received, the gift of salvation and eternal life has been bestowed. This child is fully a member of the church, but only in recent years has participation in the Lord's Supper been granted. Roman Catholics began the custom early in the twentieth century. The Orthodox Church, feeds the newly baptized infant the sacrament. This seems more logical than the practice of Christian groups who call baptism the basic rite of initiation but do not admit all baptized persons to the Lord's Table.

So far as day-to-day family life is concerned, children who have been baptized seem no different from those who have not. They continue to learn about God and the relationship to God through family relationships and religious practices. For some children, however, the next stage beyond baptism is that time when, with their families, they receive special preparation for admittance to the Lord's Table. Usually this preparation takes the form of a curricular unit that gives meaning to the rite in terms they can understand: celebration, thanksgiving, or a family meal.

Eventually there comes a time of personal commitment. Here is where the two streams diverge: Those who practice infant baptism are usually content to assume that these children have been nurtured in the Lord, and that their decision is to join the church, or to be confirmed (a word that means strengthened, referring to the action of the rite rather than the decision of the person). Such a decision may, in fact, be a deep religious experience for the individual, but is not a necessary expectation. For some the rite itself will be the moment of deepest experience. Usually there is a time of preparation. Some denominations encourage a two- or three-year period in which there is a study of Christian doctrine, the meaning of the Christian life, the understanding of prayer and worship, and reflection on the baptismal vows now to be taken upon oneself personally. Doctrinally, it means that the individuals become incorporated fully into the church, although in practice they may not see themselves as being treated differently than they were earlier. The age of confirmation among Christian denominations in the United States and Europe today varies from eight to eighteen. Usually only adults are permitted to participate in real decision making in congregational life, despite recent emphasis among some denominations on the role of adolescents in the church. Presbyterians, for example, will permit any young person to hold a church office if the congregation so desires.

Although the personal sense of commitment is frequently not probed by those in churches receiving children into membership after infant baptism, there are good reasons for noting that such a personal response can take place. The earliest nurture and education of the child encourages participation through story, drama, music, worship, the celebration of holidays, relationships, and so on.

Through methods such as story telling the child is placed in the situation of biblical people who heard the word of God spoken to them with the invitation to respond. The child identifies with Amos, Isaiah, and Jeremiah, all of whom hesitated to accept the call to speak for God to their people. The hearer of the story is like Bartimaeus needing to be healed of blindness or Peter denying the Lord. We are even among those who shouted "Crucify him," a fact uncomfortably called to mind in those congregations where the Passion story is read in dialogue on Good Friday. We may be the rich young ruler, Matthew, or Paul. Every person is called, and everyone in some way responds. It is the question asked the disciples, "Who do *you* say that I am?"

In seeking confirmation or church membership, a person, child or adult, is responding, as did those first believers, with "I believe that Jesus Christ is the Son of God and Savior." To affirm that is to accept his call to a special kind of life, practised in many settings, and continually reinforced through membership among his people, the church. The encounter with God in Christ leads to the decision, and results in the appropriation of the Christian faith as one's own. To be able to do this is a sign of self-awareness and self-identity. Having heard Jesus speak, the Samaritans said to the woman from the well: "It is no longer because of your words that we believe, for we have heard for ourselves" (John 4:42). When people "hear for themselves" their decision is no longer an affirmation of the faith of family, teacher, or pastor. This is God's work in each person.

No one may readily say at what age this kind of hearing will occur, because it is not an intellectual matter but a response that touches the whole self. A child's sense of commitment reflects a child's level of understanding and is complete for the child at that time. The commitment may not be final or complete. The child has yet to reach the years for the establishment of self-identity (in Erikson's phrase). During adolescence there may be a rejection of faith as part of the attempt to establish independence. It will be many years before a young person can fully comprehend the seriousness of commitment, but some aspects become clear during adolescence. For this reason, Pierre Babin has suggested that an additional time of commitment should be open to eighteen-year-olds.[5] The church of Denmark (Lutheran) has placed confirmation at the age of eighteen.

Recently James W. Fowler, a psychologist of religion, has been exploring the development of faith by designing categories that grow out of Lawrence Kohlberg's categories for moral development (see Chapter 6). He is not defining faith as belief *about* something (that is, cognitive understanding) but uses the classical Christian understanding of faith as belief *in* something. He calls it faithing,[6] and defines it as a way of knowing and interpreting. Faith, he says, is relational: first a response to the transcendent. This response strengthens relationships to persons and things in the world and means that faith has both an outer, or interpersonal, and an inner structure. When a person becomes incorporated into a group, his or her personal life becomes related to the expectations of others. For Fowler the infant has an undifferentiated faith. Preschool children have an intuitive projective faith based on knowing by feeling. This includes a sense of the magical, as Piaget earlier pointed out.

The second stage of faithing is called the mythic/literal. This stage is concrete. The young child accepts the authority of parents and teachers who explain the meanings of religious faith. The third stage is called the synthetic/conventional. Religion is learned from home, school, church, and peers. Children will take cues for faith from any or all of these sources. Fourth is the individuating/reflexive stage. In adolescence there is a shift to self-interpretation. Institutional religion is perceived as too conventional, and young people feel drawn to forms of religion different from the ones in which they have been nurtured. This stage gives way to the polar/dialectic. The adult reappropriates the past and makes it part of his or her personal history. Moral-volitional affirmations are made. Lastly, the universalizing stage is that of a fully-integrated faith, but Fowler sees this as a rare occurrence.

In Fowler's system, as in those of other developmentalists, it is possible for persons to stop at any stage, or to regress to an earlier one. You know adults whose faith includes elements of magic. You know others whose faith is affirmed by a literal interpretation of scripture. Some combine elements from many sources into what seems to be a syncretistic religion. Others seek a form of religion different from that in their own background. Fowler does not say that these are qualitative stages, or that the mature adult will reach the fifth stage, but it would be easy to read this into his essay. If this were implied, he, like Kohlberg, would be elevating a philosophy of religious belief into a developmental system. Only further research and writing will illumine this point. In the context of what has been said, however, notice that the point of commitment would be at stage five, that of the reappropriation of the past with moral-volitional affirmations.

Born Again

The affirmation that the Christian must be "born again" is another developmental view of faith. It combines maturation with environment. Proponents would say that God works through people, and the human communities of family and church nurture children in the Christian experience until they are able to make a personal confession of faith. This decision could be arrived at so quickly that the moment is almost, if not completely, imperceptible. It might be a sudden flash of insight (as the apostle Paul felt a blinding light), or a voice (as Augustine heard it), or "the heart strangely warmed" that John Wesley recorded. For some it has come after anguish, struggle, and resistance to the call. The poet Francis Thompson wrote of the "hound of heaven," whom at first he fled. Others describe release from a deep sense of sin and guilt. Such descriptions come from adults, most of whom had considered themselves Christians for many years prior to the event.

Can such an experience come to children? Is it essential? As was observed earlier, this kind of experience was sought, and still is, for children in some religious communities. The persistence of wrongdoing is explained as a result of original sin. It is pointed out that children are lost in sin and helpless. They are warned that they can never be with God in heaven unless their heart is changed. They must submit to God who loves them and receive Jesus Christ as their only savior. This approach to decision making is conveyed through specific techniques. Nineteenth-century books suggested that the child be impressed with the fearsomeness of dying in sin, and that this be contrasted with the love and forgiveness God was offering. The concern of parents and Sunday school teachers for the child's eternal salvation would also be a factor. By the act of submission the child would be able to please both God and parents.

The International Child Evangelism Association, Inc., was organized in 1935 in fulfillment of the belief of its founder that he had been called to work for the salvation of children. The basis for his call was a reading of Matthew 18:1–4, which he interpreted to mean that children were lost. Evangelism precedes nurture, he affirmed, and can be brought about as early as the age of three (eight years or younger being ideal) through the child's awareness of specific acts of sin.

Many evangelicals prefer to build on the spiritual climate of home and church. Their emphasis is on a response to the love of God. In a culture where comparatively few children face death, the factor of punishment is not so acute an incentive as it would be where mortality rates are high. Guilt can better be aroused by impressing on the child the love of God and how God sorrows because of the child's sin. Stress is laid on the love that Jesus showed in giving up his life on the cross to atone for sin. A doctrine of the atonement is an important element in bringing about the conversion experience. The cross symbolizes many things, including obedience, suffering, love, overcoming evil, and paying the price of sin. Christ is the ransom by which the sinner is freed; he is the substitute for those who have sinned; he is the example of moral perfection. These classical interpretations of the atonement were first enunciated by the theologians Irenaeus, Anselm, and Abelard, respectively.

Conversion means literally to be turned around (or to turn around), to have a change of mind. In Christian terms conversion has meant seeing the crucified Christ in such a way that one's own sinful nature and practice are revealed, and one is led to remorse and repentance. This is followed by the assurance of God's forgiveness and grace to live the new life. The risen Lord is the one who gives eternal life.

The Bible is the key to bringing about this awareness. Bible stories are included among the earliest books read to young children. The teacher or parent impresses the child with the way God speaks through his Word, gives examples through the lives of biblical people, and teaches rules for living. They share their own religious experience in the hope that the child will accept Jesus Christ as personal savior. Usually no pressure is put on the child, in the belief that this is the work of the Holy Spirit and will happen in God's time. Nurture provides an environment for conversion.

Whenever a child has experienced conversion and is ready to make this confession of faith in Christ, he or she will be baptized and become a member of the church. This should mean that baptism would take place throughout the year and include children of all ages. Those who affirm believers' baptism, as Gideon C. Yoder points out,[7] have not fully answered the question as to why a group of eight- (or ten-, or twelve-) year-olds will make this decision at Easter each year. Clearly there is a tendency for older children to interact with one another and be influenced in decision making by their peers and families. It could also be, as some assert, that there is a "right" (or, in educational terms, a teachable) moment, a point at which the grace of God can enter a human life with easiest cooperation.

Lewis J. Sherrill, in *The Struggle of the Soul*,[8] saw a parallel between religious development and the psychological development outlined by Erikson. He asserted that there were particular turning points in life when people were tempted to turn back to an easier, simpler level but were being called to a new phase of maturity. God draws near in these moments of struggle and temptation. Such life crises occur at about the age of six upon entering childhood, at twelve on the threshold of adolescence, at eighteen to twenty-one upon entering adulthood, and at the points of entering middle age and old age. If there is validity in Sherrill's assertion, how one teaches a child about God and the relationship to God at the age of six are important in religious development. What one does about commitment at the age of twelve and at eighteen will be strategic. Traditional Protestant evangelism has been centered on children at the ages of eight to ten as the time when the work of conversion would be most fruitful. Those who have worked with children at this age know that they are curious, open to learning, and eager to please. But it is not a turning point.

Roman Catholic children have not been directed toward this kind of religious experience. From the age of seven, when they are first admitted to the Eucharist, they receive assurance that, although sin is part of the human condition, repentance will always bring pardon. The rite of penance, now frequently delayed until later years and sometimes observed as a community rite, is a verbal and dramatic representation of God's action. It includes the assurance of forgiveness and offers ways of making amends for wrongdoing. This is an act of reconciliation and renewal.

The Significant Event

Significant events of life are always remembered. Some people remember the moment they fell in love or the day on which they pledged love to each other. They remember the day they made a decision to accept a job, met one who became a lifelong friend, "fell in love with" a community, or decided to change their lifestyle. The decision to confess Christ as Lord, to commit life to his way, and to submit one's will to the loving purposes of God is so radical that it would always be remembered. That may be why autobiographical writings describing conversion experiences usually come from adults such as St. Augustine and John Wesley. They were old enough to reflect upon their experience. A Christian community that hesitates to recognize this kind of experience may be blind to the message of the Bible. People really want to give themselves to someone or something. Some young Americans today are seeking in Eastern forms of religion a radical simplicity of lifestyle and an awareness of the transcendent that they were never taught to find within their Jewish or Christian faiths.

This way of commitment differs from the first one described in that it does not accept gradual growth in faith as sufficient. It differs from the second in not accepting a radical sense of sin and guilt as the only basis for decision and commitment. The reality of the love and presence of God can come upon a person with overwhelming power, but it is a gentle, gracious power. When love responds to love, the event is memorable and joyous. It brings a sense of unworthiness—who is ever worthy of love received? But this is not the same as guilt. This is a converson from self-awareness to self-transcendence, a turning beyond self toward God. It makes possible more mature relationships with other people, more complete acts of service, and a deeper sense of responsibility in the understanding of what it means to confess Christ as Lord.

Those who make such a commitment early do so on whatever level they are capable. God made people to develop by an internal "timetable" and does not expect ten-year-olds to act like twenty-year-olds, spiritually or in any other way. However, it is as possible to be precocious in the spiritual life as in the intellectual life. Unfortunately, some Christians never go beyond the ten-year-old sense of commitment. Their world enlarges, but their belief in God, their understanding of his purpose for them and for the world, remains childlike.

The remembrance of a first moment of commitment does not preclude later reaffirmations of faith. Churches in a liturgical tradition are recovering an interpretation of the baptismal service as a time for the already baptized, while witnessing the event for others, to reaffirm their own vows.

The place of participation in the Lord's Supper is another question that arises in connection with decision and baptism. Historically, the rite of baptism has admitted a person to the Lord's Table. Churches practicing believers' baptism would logically reserve the rite as a special part of the reception into membership. Some who see children as part of the community because of their family relationship (or their own participation if families do not attend) have admitted them because the Lord's Supper is their celebration of worship. The theology of the Lord's Supper held by a particular community of faith determines how that community views the relationship of baptism to participation in its communion rite. Where the Lord's Supper is understood to be a memorial meal, it has the aspect of teaching. Where it emphasizes the atonement, it is tied in with repentance. Where it is looked upon as a celebration with the risen Lord (and this has been prominent in recent eucharistic theology), the elements of praise and thanksgiving are stressed. Those who baptize children in infancy and expect the personal confession at the onset of adolescence have recently been admitting them between the ages of seven and ten, usually after preparation as to the meaning of the sacrament. It is affirmed that this participation, especially in churches where the Eucharist is the principal service each Sunday, is an aid toward their eventual personal commitment.

The question of the age for commitment brings into focus the understanding of the nature of religious faith, nurture, and education. A strong cognitive component within Protestantism has resulted in an insistence that children understand certain material, biblical, doctrinal, or didactic, before they are presumed capable of participating in significant religious events. In contrast, Jewish and Catholic practice has tended to involve children in significant rites at an early age and to interpret during or after the events. They are saying that inner knowing, or feeling, is essential. When this feeling is one of joy, there will be happy memories that lead to continued participation.

Such preparation comes through homes and churches where children are shown human love and are assured, by words and deeds, of God's love. It is helped by an openness to questions and to the "teachable moment" for verbally pointing to God's actions in life. It is important that the biblical story be told along with stories from two thousand years of the continuing history of those who have made the commitment and followed in the way. The ways that parents deal with wrongdoing, convey forgiveness, and are steadfast in love are important components in the conversion process. Family and church should both be involved in the preparation for baptism, confirmation, and participation in the Lord's Supper, not simply by intellectual explanation but through sharing of personal meanings. An evangelical who is sensitive to child evangelism says that children should never be asked publicly to make a decision, because some will do so either to please the asker or under a feeling of public pressure. The idea may be suggested in the Sunday school class or by personal conversation. Further conversation may be indicated, but one should be sensitive to the right moment. The wise adult stands by, ready to counsel, but awaiting the initiative of the child.[9]

Through two thousand years of Christian history, there has never been any consensus as to a specific form that the conversion experience would take. I have described three basic approaches. Perhaps no human ever fully knows what another human means standing before a congregation and, in answer to the question, "Do you accept Jesus Christ as your Lord and Saviour?" saying "I do, God being my helper."

The power to witness to Christ is a work of grace. It is, as the apostle Paul long ago pointed out, God's doing and not our own.

CHAPTER 8

Religious

Development

and the Family

O N C E upon a time it was easy to define a family. A tribe is a large family, and it still exists in nomadic cultures. The family group of three or four generations was economically useful in an agrarian society. Through the centuries the unit has become smaller. Today the mutual support available through such interrelationships has been given up in favor of the relative independence of the nuclear family consisting of parent(s) and child(ren.) The church has lived with this nuclear family model for a long time but has largely ignored the varieties of family situations in which children live. There are many one-parent families, yet most church programs and materials imply an involvement of two parents. This is evident in word and picture. When one parent brings up a child or children, a balance develops in this person between "mothering" and "fathering" modes, insofar as either can be considered distinctive. The variety of ages and relationships represented among church families could be helpful to such parents.

Divorce has been a factor in American family life for a long time, but churches seldom reflect on its implications for children. Children may be more realistic than their elders. Some feel a special status in having two families, and in being able to visit their "other family" at special times. Such children have gone through a crisis, just as their parents have. The tensions that lead eventually to divorce may weigh more heavily on a child than adults realize. There is a time after remarriage (for children whose parent has died as well as those whose parents have divorced) when the establishment of a new relationships brings tensions. Children are resilient, but change can still be difficult. How will the words *parent* and *child* be interpreted in teaching these children? How will biblical family imagery be interpreted? These terms evoke varied responses even for children growing up in traditional households. Although teachers are aware that the patterns of family life vary, their understanding is not always clear in the class. Teachers may be personally sensitive to the situations of individual children but unable to utilize this sensitivity in teaching the varieties of family life characteristic of the culture.

The Family and Religion

Whatever its composition, the family is usually the place where children are first introduced to religion. There is a spontaneous quality about it. At Christmas Santa Claus images are supplemented with a manger scene. Some families have a simple ceremony as the children put the small figures into place. The family joins with the throngs on Easter Day, gathering in church to celebrate the resurrection of Christ. Even the youngest child can feel the joy of the occasion, heightened by flowers, colors, and the triumphant shout of hymns. No matter how secularized a holy day becomes in popular observance, the religious community can reclaim the full meaning through worship and celebration.

There are family ways through which a child is introduced to religious observances. Some families continue the ancient practice of giving thanks for a meal. This elemental gesture has been universally practiced among religious groups, and its decline within the Christian tradition signals another form of secularization. Gratitude is offered to the Creator for the food that sustains life. Nowhere is this expressed with more simple reverence than in the Jewish blessing in one of its several forms: "Blessed be thou, O Lord, King of the Universe, who has caused the earth to yield food for all."

The other uniquely familial way in which children are introduced to religious practice is through the near-universal custom of teaching a child a bedtime prayer. The moment before sleep is a time for quiet and relaxation. It is also a time when fears of the dark or uncomfortable remembrances of the day may come into focus. The assurance that God is near —loving, forgiving, and protecting—is comforting, however little the child may understand the specific words or action. Something in the voice and manner of parents who pray with the child conveys the reality. Thanksgiving for love experienced through the day is reassuring.

The religious understanding of children is enriched when religiously oriented books and recordings are included among play materials. Simple biblical verses and narratives are succeeded by longer stories as the child grows. Other stories tell about people who lived their convictions or explore relationships enriched by a religious dimension. Sunday school teachers find that enriching home experiences are reflected in class. A nearby library may include religious books in the collection. A church should keep such a collection for children to borrow and teachers to use.

Television programs can broaden experience not only through specifically child-oriented programs but through general programs to be watched and interpreted in the family. A serious puppet presentation of Bible stories for children would retain the universal character without the overdramatized interpretations that commercial productions usually show. Children will view Bible spectaculars, and families will need to explain their exaggerations. In seeking to be impressive, these extravaganzas lose the awesome simplicity of the ways in which God deals with his people and may completely miss the sense of mystery so essential in any human attempt to interpret God's action. Watch the television schedule, especially at Christmas and Easter. There may be archeological documentaries that will help older children understand biblical times and places. Family conversation is important. Understand the values presented and be aware of how your children are responding. Give them the opportunity to test this presentation of life with the way they experience it as Christians in families and in the life of the church.

Inevitably, who we are teaches more profoundly than anything we do. The basic biblical image of God is that of husband, with Israel as wife. Here is the essential bond, made by mutual choice, sustained by love, tested by unfaithfulness, secured because of the unfailing forgiveness of God. The relationships that humans build in marriage reflect the divine image and affirm one of the earliest words of the Bible: that they two may become one flesh, an image quoted later by Jesus. There will be tensions as two people interweave their lives, finding a balance between independent self-affirmation and interdependent mutuality. How this balance develops is important for the growth of children, their understanding of male-female relationships, and their understanding of God. Parents who try to pretend good relationships do not succeed. Children are aware of the emotional climate in a family. Parents who work through the weaknesses and failures, joys and strengths of being human, affirming the enabling grace of God, teach on a realistic level.

Parental relationships with children constitute another factor in religious development. The "ideal parent" does not exist. Good relationships develop through the way tensions are acknowledged and resolved. People can only show anger where there is trust; they do not test a relationship of which they are not sure. The child who can say *no*, emphatically, is certain that such rebellion will make no difference in parental love. The parent can know that an angry response to such resistance will not make the child fearful. Not that anger is a useful way to cope with a situation, but if the feeling is there it is better expressed in words than in deeds. What a child needs from a parent is a feeling of security. The child needs the freedom to grow at an individual pace, encouraged, helped, and sometimes left alone.

Other relationships tell the child that life is good. Wider family relationships can be maintained even through infrequent visits among families who live at a distance from each other. Neighbors provide opportunities for children to learn how to be sensitive to people, with different expectations of what good behavior is. Brothers and sisters give children their first experience of peer relationships.

Church and Family

Formed by the elements in family living, a child enters into the life of the church. Some come as infants, joyously carried in parental arms for dedication or baptism. The child is named within the family of the church, as parents give thanks and promise to bring this one up to love and serve God. The congregation pledges support to the family in the task. This says two things: The family is responsible for the religious education of children, and the church is expected to undergird it. How can this be done?

The first responsibility is to help parents in their life together. Instruction offered parents by the pastor in preparation for the dedication or baptism of a child is important, opening possibilities both for their own religious development and that of the child. Many kinds of group experience are available, such as marriage enrichment conferences, cursillo, or forms of transactional analysis and other interpersonal relation techniques.[1] Some are designed to help couples, others are for individual development. The Roman Catholic Church has long had pre-Cana and Cana conferences for those about to be married or recently married.

Some learning opportunities are specifically geared to religious development for the whole family. This can be an especially important emphasis today. The church is the only institution in our society that includes people of all ages. Few families include three generations. One third of all Americans are single—widowed, divorced, or never married. Many among them desire the dimension of life that comes from interaction with people of other ages. Single parents can find their children's lives, as well as their own, enriched by regular participation in a group with parents of the other sex. Migratory life patterns leave many families living far from grandparents. Grandparents in a parish will enjoy occasional association with their children's generation as well as with young children. Small children will enjoy the comforting presence of surrogate grandparents. In this way the church can help people experience the extended family. It is a visible witness to the church as the family of God.

The family cluster is a way of providing this kind of intergenerational contact.[2] Families and single persons are grouped into a small teaching-learning unit meeting at specified intervals either at the church or in a home. The session usually begins with a meal, followed by worship and study. Children of varied ages are included. Biblical study might begin in story form with an emphasis on what it could mean for each person. Experience-oriented discussion would touch on common problems. Human relationships are similar for people of all ages; children's school situations parallel many that adults find at work. A cluster might explore understandings of the church, its worship and mission. The experience together could be a valuable way of developing a mutual support group and demonstrating that people in a church care about one another. Through the meal, conversation, and worship, people learn to know one another.

Another form of family gathering occurs at an all-church event such as a supper. In this larger group there can be a variety of programs, such as a film or filmstrip, slides shown by members, a dramatically told story, or a brief drama in reader's theater style. Biblical study is another possible focus. After a passage has been read aloud, the pastor would give background material. Discussion would center on the meaning for people today. Here is a way for church families to meet informally, learn, share views, and worship together. Occasionally it can be helpful to separate on an age-level basis for awhile after the initial presentation so young children can have an activity geared to their abilities while adolescents and adults explore a theme in other ways. This permits action-oriented work by children while allowing older group members to pursue ideas.

Other opportunities to share together as church families come through picnics, conferences, workdays, and family camping. One value in such events is that parents can come with their children. Do not overlook the importance of giving families opportunities to be together at home, as well. Despite the ways families are kept *together* at church, the church must be one of the worst offenders in the community for separating families evening after evening, while one or another parent attends a meeting. A Mormon strategy should become better known to other parts of the religious community. Mormons structure one evening a week as family evening,[2] on which no other church events are held. Materials are published to suggest activities that will make it an enjoyable time together at home.

One remembers that the Seder, the Passover celebration, is centered in the family. The greeting of the Sabbath on Friday evening is a special celebration among Jewish families as the mother lights the candles with a blessing and the father blesses the cup of wine. Christians do not have many such liturgical events structured into their family life. Such, however, could be developed and become customary through use.

Family workshops in preparation for holiday seasons become useful. A getting-ready-for-Christmas evening when each family makes an Advent wreath or calendar can be fun for all participants. A family liturgy for lighting the Advent candle each Sunday can be used in any home. The parish can gather one evening for making decorations, learning carols, and introducing people to the meaning of the season. A

Lenten family evening might explore approaches to this season, stressing simplicity of life without rigid (and sometimes meaningless) disciplines. An event could be structured around meditation on the way of the cross as preparation for the joy of Easter. Participants could inquire into the meaning of such words as *atonement, reconciliation, resurrection,* and *new life.*[3]

The Church Meeting Family Needs

Parents have some needs with reference to the religious education of their children that the church can meet. They need to know what curriculum is planned for the year and how they can help their child learn. Such an introduction can be provided at the beginning of the year through both a letter that gives brief explanatory information and an occasion when parents and teachers can meet to talk about mutual hopes and expectations. The minister needs to be present at such a gathering, because here is the one person professionally prepared to help laity understand biblical and theological concerns. Have someone from the religious education committee present so that parents can know what this group is doing and can voice their concerns.

Throughout the year parents need to be kept informed, and their questions encouraged. They want to know how they can be helpful. Sometimes they would welcome specific assignments for children to complete at home. Teachers could program this into the course. A Sunday absence can become a time for encouraging parental help; for instance, by suggesting reading or a make-up assignment. If a child is ill, an activity is welcome. If a child is out of town, a home assignment will help him or her to keep up with the class. Parents make good resource persons in specific areas of competence and can be invited as occasional helpers or asked to be hosts for class social events.

Parents should be offered opportunities to further their own learning.[4] Many are aware that they still have a childish knowledge of the Bible and that they really have not thought much about basic Christian understandings. Some will find time to learn if their needs are kept in mind and their schedules respected. Some have free mornings on which they might attend classes. While they are in class, their young children can play in the preschool room. Adult Sunday morning classes could provide such opportunities. Some parents are willing to employ a baby-sitter while they attend an evening class. These must be short-term courses, four to six weeks in length, as few people will commit themselves longer. An evening or a short-term course could be built on the theme of the religious development of children or the family and Christian education. The specific subjects are not so primary as encouraging parents to explore biblical and theological foundations for their own religious growth.

Parents are the first teachers of religion, but they can only teach out of the fullness of their personal understanding. That is why it is essential that they take this task seriously. They are growing, and their understandings will continue to develop. One can never assume that because children think simply, it does not matter how little parents or teachers know. They are conveying attitudes. This appears in remarks that children hear: "They must have been doing something wrong," or "Yes, I think the dog will go to heaven." Parents evidence their own religious understandings in the attitudes they take toward other religious groups and in how they encourage their children to relate to others. Knowing and appreciating the religious customs, forms of belief, and liturgical practice of their friends can be an enriching experience for children. Parents will encourage or discourage this by their own expressed awareness of the wideness of God's love toward all his children.

Attitudes are also conveyed indirectly. Adults express how they feel about large numbers of new people moving into the community, whether from overseas, rural, or city areas. It is important to try to understand the contribution new people can make and find ways of welcoming them to church and community, aware that changes will come because of their presence. Parental attitudes will influence a child's ability to relate to new environments or to withdraw from the possibility of change. People vary in their feelings about families deprived of adequate means for living. Some, lacking the biblical capacity for compassion, believe suffering is their own fault. When parents are able to become involved in constructive ways of building community, a child's understanding of the meaning of the Christian faith and life will develop in this context. Adult responses to political and social issues are reflected in words as well as in deeds. Other influences come to the child through neighborhood friends, school, and church. The family opinions that children bring to the church school class become a basis for exploring the variety of options for Christian approaches to living.

Parental attitudes toward and relationships to the church are also influential. Today most children are dependent upon parents for transportation. This has made many churches family-oriented. Some children are left off for the Sunday school session and called for afterwards. This indicates parental concern for the child's religious education. Such children are as much a part of the church community as those whose parents are active participants. In other families activities seem to revolve around the children until the children wonder if there is any time when parents are alone together at home. The most important event for parents should be to attend the church service with their children. This should be considered one obligation they assume at the dedication or baptism of their children. Frequently, however, the ceremony is considered a social or family event, without any feeling of responsibility for continuing the process.

Children should feel welcome to the church at birth. Many community agencies offer assistance to prospective and new parents; the church should appoint one person to welcome the family and offer materials to help with the first steps in religion. Such a person could answer questions, suggest activities, and learn parental needs. An invitation can be extended to join in a group with other parents, or help offered so that parents will be able to go to an outside meeting. If the church has a nursery or a class for the youngest children, its teacher would be a potential home visitor. When children regularly attend Sunday school, the teacher becomes a contact person with families to help them relate comfortably to the whole life of the church.

Church and family have interlocking responsibilities for the religious nurture of children. Parents want to know how they can help. The church should be equally alert to know its task and fulfill it.

CHAPTER 9

The Child

in the Christian

Community

M O S T Christians bring their children into the church in infancy. This expresses the parents' acknowledgment of the child as a gift of God, their thanksgiving for this new life, and their desire that the child shall grow in faith. In many traditions the time of baptism is when the child is brought under the new covenant, affirmed in the new life in Christ. The parents assume certain promises on behalf of the child and are committed to nurture the child so that these promises will be personally acknowledged at an age of responsibility.

Children and Worship

Community worship is at the heart of the church's life. The Sunday gathering is a weekly celebration of the resurrection of the Lord. Children belong here. They can understand the expressions of praise, thanksgiving, and joy. This does not mean that they should be expected to be present every week and attend the full service; their participation will vary according to their age and individual needs. Some children can sit quietly for a longer time than others. Some are able to understand the words at an earlier age than others. Children in small churches may feel closer to the action and more involved than do children in large churches. Being present with parents makes a difference. When children are among adults they find it easier to follow the pattern than when they are with other children. The unfortunate habit of squeezing a number of children into one pew in order to keep a class together seems to promote mostly discomfort.

Anyone who participates in a service of worship is learning about God and at the same time expressing relationship to God. This makes worship an important way through which children grow in faith. A service should be filled with joy and thanksgiving. Hymns express this; children feel more closely identified with the service when they learn hymns and can join in singing.

Scripture is an integral part of worship: hearing the word of God spoken to his people. Sometimes the reading will be far from the personal experience of children, and their attention will wander. Teachers and parents need to provide a time for explaining the scripture lesson. If the class session comes before the church service, teachers could look at the readings in advance, and tell the story or share an important verse. If the class comes after the service, the teacher can take time to look up passages in the Bible and help children recall what they have heard.

The sermon or homily is basically an explanation of scripture and its application to life. It is one way that the good news of the gospel is proclaimed. The sermon is planned for adults, who make up most of the congregation. They expect spiritual sustenance from it, and for many it may be their only form of religious education. Older girls and boys may find some of it comprehensible, depending on the subject matter, style, and length.

Many people are familiar with the so-called children's sermon. It is rarely a real sermon, although this could be helpful if a preacher, sensitive to children, explored one of their life concerns in practical terms, assuring them of God's presence and giving them a biblical story or passage. It could also be helpful if the time were used for real story telling, with well-written material and the narration carefully prepared, using biblical, biographical, historical, or contemporary material. Adults would benefit as much as the children. The one thing preachers should not do (but frequently do) is to give object lessons. Young children think concretely and do not make abstract deductions from a concrete example. Piaget's studies (see Chapter 2) indicate that children think concretely until the age of almost twelve. But the whole point of the object lesson is to make an abstraction from the concrete. The teller shows children something that will hold their attention, then tells them that God (or the Bible or the Christian life) is like that object. At best they will be confused. Usually they will forget the explanation almost immediately and remember only the object. What a waste of time—unless entertainment was the whole point!

For example, a minister sees a connection between a map and a Bible: each is a guide. Now children can understand what a map is, but they cannot see how the Bible is like a map. The Bible is a book. The map tells you how to get some place. They watch it being used when the family is traveling. They can further understand that the Bible is a book that tells about God, and that it tells how God wants people to live. But the connection between traveling to grandparents' house and traveling the road that God sets is a confusing one. One possible parallel might relate to child experience. The minister could share how a map is used for traveling and ask if they have seen maps so used. When information on travel is needed, this is what one uses. Showing a Bible, the minister might then affirm that when one wants to know about God's love, or how God wants us to live, one turns to the Bible. But why bother to make such a roundabout connection? Why not just talk about the Bible in the first place and give the illustration by reading from it?[1]

Prayer is a primary way people learn to express their relationship to God. As God speaks to his people through scripture, so they respond in prayer. Children can understand this more easily through some forms of prayer than through others. Brevity, not length, holds their attention and makes comprehension more possible. The litany form with the people's response gives both pause and a change. Expressions of thanksgiving for the many experiences of life speak to children. Some of the concerns expressed through intercession may be beyond the knowledge of younger children, but teaching broad enough to keep them alert to needs outside themselves is preparing them for fuller participation.

Even the youngest children know the meaning of doing wrong, the struggle to feel sorry, the desire to be forgiven, and the satisfaction in the restoration of relationships. The prayer of confession expresses these needs. Some forms have words simple enough for a child to understand. More complicated traditional forms will be beyond their comprehension.

Participation in Worship

More frequent participation in the Lord's Supper has become increasingly the pattern and practice in recent years. Some Protestant churches that, in the past, might have observed this rite quarterly or bimonthly have tended to do so monthly, with additional celebrations for special events. The dramatic simplicity is itself a form of teaching. Participants cannot help but become involved. Some forms of the liturgy stress the action more than others, as the presiding minister lifts the cup and breaks the bread. In all forms the people become involved when they go forward to receive these gifts or share them with one another.

When children's involvement in worship is planned, they will join the congregation for specific portions of the service. It might be to participate in the early part, sharing in hymn and scripture, be present for the celebration of the Lord's Supper, or witness a baptism. On the great feast days, Christmas, Easter, and Pentecost, they will probably share in the full celebration. Their participation is enhanced when they understand what is going on. This is a responsibility of the church school class as well as the family. Children can learn some hymns (the organist may be a resource person); they can be taught how to read psalms and other responses. Children need to get the "feel" of how to engage in responsive reading. The class can practice reading, using simple psalms, and parts of psalms. Children can memorize responses that will be used in the service and learn to sing responses that are used frequently, such as the *Gloria Patri, Doxology, Sanctus,* and others.

One church school teacher realized that the children were never in the service at the time of passing the peace. This was an act children could understand, but because (in this service) it came after the sermon and before the offertory, they missed it no matter for which half of the service they were present. They learned the responses in class and rather timidly practiced extending hands to one another. One Sunday they attended this part of the church service. When adults nearby reached out toward them, they felt in a new way the warmth that is within the Christian community when someone said, "The peace of the Lord be with you."

Preparing for Worship

It is not enough simply to teach children how to participate in the service of worship. They also need to be able to use materials that express worship in language and ideas within their experience. This can be accomplished through services planned specifically for children. Nursery children could offer a simple prayer of thanksgiving before juice and crackers are shared. A simple song of thanksgiving (some will be found in children's hymnals and other teaching resources) could be followed by a few sentences of prayer that express thanks for experiences the group has been sharing. Kindergarten children will need a similarly informal service. It will be possible to use with them brief biblical passages expressing in a few verses praise, thanks, and assurance; this is the way they learn that hearing the scriptures is part of meeting together for worship. Some teachers like to include a simple story, but this may be better saved for later in the session when it can more easily be incorporated into conversation. It could, however, form a transition into other elements of the session.

Children of early elementary age also need materials geared to their own expression in worship. The "order" of service changes little: sentences to call them to worship, hymn, scripture, and prayer. The leader may wish to give a brief introduction to scripture and invite conversation after it has been heard. An offertory may be included because these children are old enough to have some understanding of why money is brought and how it is used. They do not yet fully understand this as a form of worship. There is too much symbolism in the idea of offering. A concrete offering is illustrated in traditions where the bread and wine are brought forward during the offertory and then used for the Lord's Supper. The connection is obvious. But presentation of money that will be used later in other ways requires more subtle thinking. Preparatory conversation may help because at least it will let the teacher know how the children are thinking.

Older elementary children will participate in the worship of the congregation more frequently. Their worship together could be a brief version of the full service. There will be opportunity to pray together at the beginning or close of the teaching session to express thanks for being together, a desire to learn and grow toward God, and intercession for particular needs, binding the group together. Individuals should feel free to participate vocally or to remain silent, and all can learn by the practice of silence that this is a special way of feeling God's presence and of being aware of one another. The sensitivity of the teacher can make this a relaxed time where words and quiet alternate, and children deepen their own experience of prayer.

Belonging to the Church

Children are part of the church community in many ways. The psychologist David Elkind, who has been quoted earlier, asked questions to discover how children at various ages understood what it means to be members of a particular religious group.[2] Five- to seven-year-olds have an undifferentiated view of religious identity. Asked why a person might be Catholic or Protestant, a child of this age answered, "God makes you." Or they felt that religious identity was somehow bound up with national identity. Seven- to nine-year-olds are beginning to develop sharper perceptions. They know the denominations to which they belong. "How do you know?" Elkind asked. "Because I go to that church." It was that concrete. Children from ten to twelve years old are just beginning to understand why people belong to one religious group and not another. They could reflect on the question. They knew that not all children belonged to churches, and that not all were Protestant, Catholic, or Jewish. They were beginning to know something of their own beliefs and to understand, in an elementary way, what it means to be a Jew, a Catholic, or a Protestant.

It is instructive for adults to realize that words do not have the same meaning for all children, even when definitions have been explained. Familiarity with nomenclature comes as the words are used. The feeling of what it means to be part of a specific religious group comes only with time. The distinctions among Protestant groups are frequently blurred. There may be more differences within a denomination than between denominations. People who belong to numerically small religious groups are aware of their distinctiveness earlier.

The child belongs to the religious community in many ways. Some parishes seem almost to be built around families with children. The children are welcomed at many activities. People know and greet them by name. When there is a coffee hour, they mingle with others (hopefully not eating up all the cookies and trying not to run into other people). At a church supper families are highly visible. Such children feel at home. This is their church.

Other churches are less welcoming to children. They still

feel that younger ones should be segregated in the parish house. People speak sharply when a child runs by. Some are afraid that children will stand on upholstered chairs or knock over someone's coffee cup. They expect children to disrupt a quiet life, and they probably will not be disappointed. Children know when they are not wanted. However seldom this attitude may be found, it spells the end of any real community. The church, like any other family, needs people of all ages. It needs people of grandparent and great-grandparent age, it needs people of parent age, it needs children and youth. All learn the meaning of Christian concern through their interaction. Parents feel welcomed when children are. Within the church family, as in any other, it is important that people be sensitive to one another's needs, not presuming upon either indulgence or resignation toward behavior that hurts or seriously inconveniences someone else. There are times for young and old to be apart and times for them to be together. The balance may be one key to happy relationships.

Children feel most completely part of a parish when there are specific ways in which they can contribute to its life. At a summer bazaar in a country parish, the children watch over the booth at which recycled games and puzzles are sold. They are working in their own area, feel that they are helping make the event successful, and are having a good time. Mothers setting up tables for a church dinner are followed by small children contentedly placing napkins or silverware. Other children help the adults prepare the church for Christmas or Easter. No one invents occasions when there would be something for children to do; the children are included because they happen to be around when the work is being done. There is no one with whom to leave them at home, and this is gain. When children's classes meet in the parish hall, the work they do in class can be both instructional and useful, decorating the long bare walls that usually make up such rooms. People can see what is being learned, and this becomes learning material for adults.

Pastor and Children

The minister is a central person in any church community. How a person relates to children is an individual matter. Some adults are comfortable; others feel awkward. Some enjoy small children; others are more at ease with those old enough for conversation. But when a minister is comfortable with children, a special relationship develops. Parents can encourage this by inviting the pastor to their home. Children feel more comfortable with new people on familiar ground. Later when they see the minister at church, they recognize a friend and will call out a cheerful greeting.

Acquaintance in the church develops through several avenues. Children see the pastor conduct the service. Wise teachers make opportunities for the clergy to meet classes informally. When a class visits the church to study the symbols, chancel, and various objects used during the service, the minister is the person best qualified to conduct such a tour. There is specific material to explain, and the informal action of walking around the building creates opportunities to hear and respond to questions. Time can be found before or after a service, or even, if need be, at a time specifically arranged during the week.

The minister also becomes known to children through special worship events that may be structured for them. Some churches whose religious education programs change during the summer have a service in June to highlight the children's work and presence. Without this being an amateur performance where scared children speak words that no one hears, there can be a happy balance between their participation and the total framework of the service. They can sing or lead a choric reading of the psalms; older children can read the scripture lessons. Inviting them to sit informally on the floor of the chancel area while the minister speaks to them has a magnetic effect on the adults, who are both watching the children and involved themselves in the presentation.

Perhaps you plan a special Easter service on a Sunday afternoon or a Good Friday service through which children can have some understanding of the meaning of the day. No one fully appreciates Easter who has not observed Good Friday. Children can understand something of how God's love was expressed on this day. The pastor is the best person to conduct this service, although teachers and children will also be involved.

In other churches, a special Christmas Eve service may be planned for families with children. It comes early in the evening when the preparation for the holiday has been completed and just before the children would be going to bed. Familiar carols are sung. Children place the figures in the manager scene as the familiar nativity story is told. They sing for the congregation a carol learned for the occasion. Someone tells a classic Christmas story. All share in the prayer of thanksgiving for the wonderful event about to be celebrated. The service has been brief, but every word and action has been clear even to the youngest child. Maybe there is time to share cookies and the wassail bowl before the families scatter to their homes.

The Roman Catholic church has liturgies specially designed for celebrating the Eucharist with children, authorized several years ago.[3] The regular order is followed, but scripture lessons are simplified and chosen around specific themes. The canon is followed, but the wording has been simplified so that even a young child can understand. These liturgies are planned for use when children are together at school or some special event. The words are simple without being "childish" and convey the fullness of the liturgical celebrations. Churches with similar liturgies will find this pattern useful.

The ecumenical dimension is important in teaching children about participation in the life of the church. This can no longer be ignored. It may be as simple as visiting other churches to see the interior, study the usages, and meet clergy who can welcome and explain. Ecumenical awareness comes naturally when children visit other churches with friends and neighbors. Increasingly, there are joint educational opportunities: vacation schools or weekday programs. Ecumenism seems to begin at the top and work its way down. There is perceptive interaction at national and regional levels. People know each other socially within a community. But in local parishes, there may be some hesitance about sharing in learning about other religious traditions. Many have yet to learn that, by becoming acquainted with others, they learn more about their own tradition, and their loyalty is strengthened as they discover their own distinctive contribution to the whole church as well as the similarities and differences in others. One good way of encouraging such interaction is for adults to join in ecumenical study groups, pondering the biblical message together, and for teachers to study together in workshops. They will discover that all have the same problems and possibilities.

The church of which children are a part is first of all the local parish to which they and their families are linked through many familiar bonds. It extends from there to other families of the church and the community. In time children will realize that they are part of a world-encircling fellowship that extends back through the millennia.

CHAPTER 10

Ways of

Teaching

THE earlier chapters of this book have outlined how children learn—their intellectual, emotional, and religious development—and have explored the learning environments of family and church. The question is sometimes asked whether religious education is instruction or nurture. To nurture is to provide a physical and emotional environment in which a child grows and develops. To instruct is to give direct and specific teaching through which the child learns about the physical and cultural environment. There is no way that these aspects can be separated. Parents teach even while they nurture. They may watch with a child as a squirrel scurries up a tree, or explain foods on a supermarket shelf.

Teachers nurture while they instruct. Teachers in schools and churches are very important persons to whom children turn for comfort and encouragement as well as for information or direction. Developing, maturing, growing, and learning are intertwining processes in which numbers of significant people are involved: parents, teachers, peers.

Learning is what takes place in the child. In order that a child may learn, someone has to teach. Teachers (and this includes parents) have the responsibility of helping children learn. This chapter focuses on the process of teaching. Those who teach need to have a sense of personal self-awareness, an understanding of children and the ability to relate to them, knowledge of instructional materials, and teaching skills.

Jerome Bruner, a psychologist concerned with the instructional process, has outlined four intrinsic elements in a child's learning.[1]

Curiosity

To begin with, children are curious. They want to know *how,* and *what,* and *why.* The level on which they inquire varies as they develop intellectually, as we have seen earlier. A child's curiosity can be a powerful incentive to learning. It necessitates that the teacher (and this includes parent) set up situations in which curiosity will be aroused and be open to the kinds of questions and explorations through which a child will want to follow until he or she is satisfied with the results. Encouraging children's curiosity makes a lively class. It requires a flexible teacher who enjoys stimulating learning in others and does not depend on easy answers as a way of getting through a session. The child's curiosity is a motivating force in learning. The teacher's task is to stimulate that curiosity.

The Drive to Achieve Competency

Children find satisfaction as they develop competency and achieve a certain mastery of a process. Erikson outlined the development of competency as a task of middle childhood (see Chapter 1). Every day in school they are learning how to read, work with numbers, and express their thoughts through speech and writing. These skills are the basis on which learning takes place in the sciences, social studies, literature, and other fields. Teachers in religious education can make use of these skills. But do many really do so? How many teachers are aware of children's progress in reading? This skill is frequently ignored or else overestimated. As children learn to read, they want practice. First-grade children should find on the chalkboard or bulletin board a growing lexicon of words in religious usage. This is a vocabulary they will probably never learn in school. Children can extend the list week by week: altar, Bible, Christmas, all the way to Zacchaeus. The teacher can pick simple sentences from the Bible or worship service and write these on wall charts. A shelf of first readers should be available for browsing. Few publishers of religious books offer these, but they are worth searching out. Basic readers may be supplemented by reading or telling stories. Both forms of reading are needed: the children can be taught to read in unison as well as encouraged to read silently. As they develop competence, there will be more reliance on silent reading and less on reading aloud. This is the way they are learning in school, because good readers grasp whole passages and do not concentrate on individual words. Sunday schools that still have children take turns reading are setting up bad reading habits. However, taking parts in reading, so that it becomes a narrative play, may increase skills and add interest.

Writing skills are rarely used effectively in religious education. For young children this is slow work, but they persist with amazing good will until they have copied out what is asked of them. Writing can be a way of reinforcement learning; the children can hear and speak the Lord's Prayer, see it on a chart, and then write it out. They need encouragement and plenty of time. They will have real satisfaction in placing the finished writing in their learning folder.

Free composition is another skill that older children are beginning to learn. It goes beyond the ability to fill in words or do a sentence-completion exercise and involves the ability to express thoughts in whole sentences. This skill can be used as it develops. Children should be encouraged to express their thoughts and feelings. Dramatization is a good vehicle for their expression; they can "be" a biblical character and speak from that viewpoint. They can "be present" at a worship gathering of an early Christian community and describe the feeling of the congregation. They can write what Easter means to them.

Before children can combine thinking with written expression, they are able to respond orally. The tape recorder becomes a valued teaching tool. The teacher begins an informal conversation and guides it with flexibility. The ability to ask questions in a voice that does not suggest an answer is important. The teacher might ask, "How do you think about God?" and continue with questions that flow from that inquiry. Each child is given the opportunity to respond. (As a practical matter, the teacher will want to make sure of naming the child who is asked the question so that in reviewing the tape later the speaker can be identified.) At another session the tape can be played back to the class for further discussion. With the children's permission, this could also be used to help parents or teachers become sensitive to children's growing awareness.

Number work is the skill least used in religious education. It could help older children deal realistically with the church budget: the cost of maintaining the building, developing the program, helping people within the community and throughout the world. It will be useful in constructing a timeline to visualize the centuries of biblical and church history. Basic skills children have should be used to satisfy their need for concrete learning.

Through religious education programs, the church seldom teaches children to their fullest capabilities to understand the Bible and its background, the church, or the Christian lifestyle. Although children grow in the ability to think conceptually, they are not sufficiently encouraged to develop their understanding of God, deepen their knowledge of Jesus, or find fuller meaning in prayer and worship. Sunday school teachers are seldom aware of the background knowledge of human institutions supplied by social studies. When children are studying community, the church school could explore the place of churches in a community. Most children have friends in several churches. When they study about their own nation, stories and study units could explore different religious communities. As the exploration moves around the world, this could be picked up through units on the world outreach of the Christian faith. Children who have been learning biblical competency at home and have had opportunities to explore the meaning of faith with parents bring these resources into their religious education classes at church.

The Process of Identification

Children identify with the adults in their life. They learn to talk because parents talk to them. They want to be like parents and teachers and are disappointed when they do not seem able to please these people. The child is not trying to imitate adults so much as trying to absorb qualities that adults seem to feel are important. Religious habits of parents, such as prayer or attendance at worship, become part of a child's life. Attitudes that a parent expresses about God or other people become assimilated by children. When teachers want children to remain quiet in class, children will try to comply. In watching how teachers interact with other children, a child learns ways of getting along in the classroom. Teachers' feelings about God expressed in prayer with the class may be more important in a child's learning than other ways through which a teacher tries to explain who God is. Teachers' attitudes toward the Bible are shown by the way stories are told.

Teachers and parents may feel that being a model for identification in attitudes and actions is an enormous responsibility, but they need not be discouraged. They are asked only to be themselves. One may enjoy the children. Enthusiasm is contagious. A growing, deepening faith in God is important, and this should be strengthened in the worship and fellowship of the church. Parents and teachers need to be careful that their behavior reinforces the words spoken. One may not talk about God's love without showing love and care, however imperfectly. There is no point in talking about forgiveness while pretending to be perfect. Parents and teachers should feel free to be human.

Reciprocity

Finally, reciprocity is an important element in learning. Children learn by working together and find out that some things can be best accomplished through cooperation. Reciprocity does not mean that everyone does the same thing. On the contrary, it facilitates the development of individual roles and specialized skills. There is a place for many competencies. This means structuring the teaching situation so that children may help one another in learning tasks. Teachers are members of a "team," along with occasional resource persons or visitors. Understanding the learner as a person is essential. This means taking time to "feel into" the situation of a child by remembering one's own childhood as well as by observing children sympathetically. The more the teacher is aware of the needs and capabilities of children, the easier teaching will be, and the more fully the children will learn.

Good teaching engages the learner actively in the learning process because, as Skinner points out, humans are activity-oriented beings. This does not mean that physical activity is the only mode of learning. Listening can be active too. Thinking is an activity. The teacher plans, encourages, facilitates, and is a partner in the learning process. When most of the activity comes from the teacher (talking, showing, directing), there still need to be ways to discover how much the pupil has learned. When activity becomes the basis for teaching, changes in pace are important as the class session becomes structured in turn around listening, responding, talking, thinking, acting, or reflecting. Movement and variety are responses to the fact that the attention span of a young child is short. It will be longer for some children than for others, through some methods rather than others, and at some times more than at others.

Teacher Flexibility

The teacher's flexibility is an essential element in teaching. A teacher needs to be the kind of person who can accept changes and interferences, take surprises in stride, and not be made uncomfortable by deviations from a schedule. Such a person will structure a session with built-in possibilities for change: having more material and more methods than will be used in the time given; being able quickly to terminate a learning experience if the children become restless or expand another that becomes of absorbing interest; being tolerant about interruption and able to resume the session with good humor.

Flexibility includes the willingness to hear any question a child asks and deal seriously with it, not seeing this as a threat to knowledge or faith. It means being able to say that one does not know an answer but will look for it, inviting children to join in the search, and admitting mistakes. A teacher need not be confined to book questions and book answers, or to questions with factual answers ("How many books in the Bible?" "Who was the brother of Jacob?"). Teachers should acknowledge any answer and observe that all contribute to learning. Some teachers may feel uncomfortable if they use a life-situation experience to introduce a Bible story only to find that the children ignore the latter and concentrate on the former. This may indicate that, while the life situation seems real, the children do not yet see the connection with biblical persons. The story of the baby Jesus in the temple may remind a kindergarten class of the new baby at home, making them both uncomfortable and happy by the change in the family. No teachers' manual can predict the response of a class. A teacher's flexibility in responding to children's sometimes surprising reactions to material is something that develops with increasing experience and the competence such experience brings.

Flexibility is the key to arousing a child's curiosity, an important motive for learning. No one can describe to another how curiosity is aroused. It develops as a teacher increases in an understanding of children and can plan methods of teaching in accordance with the children's development. It reflects a teacher's own religious knowledge and experience, making it possible to move easily into some uncharted ways that open during the course of a session. This does not mean to give up session planning. The result could be chaos! Rather, it means to plan an order through which a session can move, with alternatives: ways of slowing down or moving more quickly, dropping a procedure as indicated, adding something if it seems a lively issue. A teacher needs first of all to be a flexible *person*.

A good teacher bases a session on exploration. The teacher is a guide who points directions, encourages searching, shares knowledge, and gives pupils freedom to follow where their curiosity leads. When a child expresses an idea or insight, this should be cause for rejoicing. If it is partly correct, a teacher can help the child complete the answer. If it is incomplete, he or she can encouragingly suggest another try. Children need to know that any idea is important, because people can learn from errors as well as from correct answers. Some children never express an idea because they are afraid of making a mistake. Someone once ridiculed them, and they concluded that, unless you are certain of an answer, it is better to remain silent. Fear blocks learning. The good teacher fields questions with enjoyment and is never shocked by children's beliefs or understandings. There is joy in searching and sharing together.

Teachers can continue to increase in knowledge, skill, and personal religious growth. Reading and practice are helpful. So are meetings and workshops where teachers share their skills, inadequacies, joys, and discouragement. Teachers need the satisfaction of having skilled people help them to increase their skills. They need help from their ministers in biblical and theological study.

The Process of Learning: Participation

There are steps to religious learning, methods for teaching, and ways of evaluating results.[2] People respond to events first as observers. Their curiosity is aroused, and they want a closer look. This is where the teacher begins. People learn when they feel themselves to be participants in events. For Christian learners this means to become participants in the gospel story as the central event of faith. This is the good news of what God has done for his people through Jesus Christ. It is the whole story of the Bible and is climaxed in the story of Jesus: his life, death, and resurrection. The word *story* is used deliberately. It does not mean fiction, as some people suppose. Biography is story. So is autobiography. These are stories of personal life. In this sense, the Bible is the story of God's work with Israel, and the gospels are the story of Jesus. Stories are absorbing and hearers become involved. Somewhere it becomes "his" or "her" story.

The gospel story is meant to be known this way. The hearer is the person who comes to Jesus saying, "I believe, help my unbelief (Mark 9:24)"; who invites him to "stay with us" (Luke 24:29); who confesses "you are the Christ "(Mark 8:29); but who also says "I do not know this man" (Mark 15:71). The hearer identifies with Mary after the resurrection, the Emmaus pilgrims who meet the risen Lord, Peter being forgiven. The hearer of the gospel is not confused with Jesus, who taught, healed, and suffered. That role is unique. The Christian is one who has been led to him and healed by him into new life.

There are many ways of learning the story. One is the ancient method of story telling where the hearers identify with people in the story. Story books retelling the narratives supplement the biblical text. Listeners are also affected by seeing films and filmstrips, listening to cassettes or records, and reading or participating in drama. Games are another way of becoming involved in a situation. The liturgy of the Lord's Supper is the basic way in which the church re-presents the story. Hymns and other musical forms tell the story.

Response

Whenever people are caught up in the story, they become aware of the call to respond. This call may be felt tentatively or as a sharp encounter. The rich young ruler did not hear it compellingly, but Saul on the road to Damascus was struck by the blinding light. In responding positively, one becomes identified with all those who, from the first hearers on, have lived their lives in joyful response to Jesus Christ. The response can be made in daily decision making or in the total direction of a life. It does not come simply from hearing and acknowledging the gospel in an intellectual way but only when a response of the whole person is made.

Another way to look at an encounter and response is in terms of perception. A person first becomes informed. If the information fits into a total experience, one perceives it in relation to the self. One says, "So that's how it is!" or "Now I understand." Abstract knowledge has become personal knowledge. A decision is made to accept this truth personally and to acknowledge the possibility that change will have to be made because of the new understanding.

One may ask what this has to do with children's learning. Only after children have understood what one is trying to teach have they really learned. When it makes a difference to them they will respond to teaching. Teaching must meet a need.

Communication

Only after learning has become internalized can it be communicated to other people. The child who has really learned a Bible story can retell it or draw a picture about it. Older children who have been reading the story or seeing a film can respond in some kind of interpretative writing. They are ready to discuss meanings. They are also reaching an age for a personal confession of faith, which should involve a clear statement of understanding.

On an adult level we speak of evangelism or outreach as a response of those who have affirmed their faith. Among children a parallel expression would be to invite friends and neighbors who had no church affiliation to attend church with them. Evangelism would mean an awareness of human need expressed through contributions to agencies involved in helping children, alleviating hunger, or encouraging sensitivity to the environment. As children study in school about other countries, they become able to feel kinship with Christians around the world, learning how they live and worship. Since children themselves are a minority and sometimes feel misunderstood, they are able to identify with the needs of other minorities. They are sensitive to justice and injustice.

Children understand the immediate more easily than the distant, but today the distant is brought instantaneously near through television. News of the world is seen each evening: war, flood, and earthquake; violence as well as joy. They are participating vicariously in the life of the world. Their Christian faith can help them to understand and respond. The Bible is not only a book of ancient stories. It speaks to people today. No teacher can neglect this factor.

Participation comes through action. Children are quick to respond to the needs of others. Over protected children are inhibited in their growing up. The violence they see on television programs does not help them either to channel aggressiveness or to develop sympathy; in fact, it could lead them to desire more violence. It would be better for them to view documentaries, sharing insights with understanding adults who can help them to deal with their feelings and respond in a positive way to human need.

Teachers can plan ways for children to act through church and community. They can learn what projects are included in the school program. Through conversation in class, teachers can discover each week what programs children have been viewing on television and what they have heard of the world news. To assure them that God's love is being shown in this world is part of the task.

Quality education has nothing to do with numbers. It comes from creative teachers backed by encouraging parents and a church that provides needed facilities. The number of children and the size of the building are not important. There could be twenty children or two hundred; one room or a multistoried educational building.

Learning Centers

The ungraded class has been the key to improved learning for some smaller churches using team teaching and learning centers. This approach has some elements of the one-room schoolhouse that few people can remember. A larger group of children meets as a class in one large room. In a small Sunday school, grades one through six could fit comfortably into such a grouping. In a medium-sized church, this could be a two- or three-grade grouping. In a very large Sunday school, a first grade that had previously been divided into several small groups (on the theory that small groups make possible more effective teaching) would be combined into one unit. The value in using three teachers with a group of twenty-four children, instead of one teacher with each group of eight children, lies in the diversity of talents, the possibility of shifting group sizes during a session, and the freedom of one teacher to work with an individual where indicated. Planning is done by a team of teachers that might include one or more adults with high-school age helpers. This allows for necessary absences that tend to occur if someone at home is sick on a Sunday morning or a family goes away for a weekend. When church school and church meet at the same hour, teachers are able to take turns attending worship. The important point is that two or more people are planning the program.

Learning centers offer a variety of methods and materials for use within any one session or unit of study. Instead of viewing the session plan as a succession of activities—story telling, followed by conversation, looking at pictures, studying Bible verses, and drawing a mural—all these possibilities will be available at the same time. A comfortable corner with rug is a reading center for books and story telling. A table with materials invites activity work. Pictures and charts are on the wall. Bibles, pencils, paper, and resource books make a study center. Whether one teacher helps at two centers or there are enough teachers for each center depends on the people available and the size of the children's group. Each child keeps a folder for completed materials, and each knows the learning assignments expected for a unit. They move from one center to another, either by choice or at a teacher's suggestion. In this way some children may do more work and some less, but each can complete tasks satisfactorily during a session.

The learning center approach can be used even in a building with small classrooms. Each room is set up as a separate center and the children who would usually make up three or four classes move freely among them.

This approach permits flexibility to meet the needs of individual children as well as to utilize the particular skills of teachers. Individuals could be invited to work with the children for a few sessions, using a particular skill, such as drama, music, or crafts. It encourages the use of high school and junior high helpers, parents, and other resource persons who can share special information because of their work in the church. Planning and teaching responsibilities are shared among a team. Finally, children are encouraged to try new skills. The slow learner is not hurried or left frustrated with an incomplete assignment. The fast learner does not sit impatiently looking for something to do.

If any public school in the community uses the learning center approach, Sunday school teachers should find time to visit. They will need to ask in advance for an appointment through the office of the school superintendent or principal. At the school, someone will explain the reasons for using learning centers and the goals teachers hope to accomplish by their use. After watching a class in action, Sunday school teachers will have some clues as to how to adapt what they see in that classroom to their own situation. I once accompanied a group of theological students on a visit to such a school. As we waited in the office for an introductory tour, we saw prominently displayed on a wall the statement, "No child is a failure." That is the reason for learning centers. It is based on the premise that every child can do something well, and it is the job of school and teachers to find out how to help each child learn. This should be a promise for those who teach children in the community of the Christian church as well. We have been called, and so have they. We are learning together and growing toward ever deeper commitment in Christ.

CHAPTER 11

The Bible

Speaks to

Children

DEVELOPMENTAL categories can be applied to many areas of a child's life. Ronald Goldman, working in England, where biblical material may be and is taught in nonchurch schools, did some research in this area. He asked about the cognitive understandings children derive from learning biblical stories. His goal was to find a basis on which to choose biblical material for use with children. He chose three biblical stories, told them to children of different ages, and recorded how they understood each story.

Explaining Bible Stories

The first narrative was that of Moses and the burning bush.[1] Asked, "How do you explain that the bush did not burn up?" children of ages six to eight replied, "God might be throwing water on it," or "God was inside the bush and he was holding the fire up on sticks from inside," or "It might have been imitation flames like bits of red paper stuck on the bush." From about nine years on the ideas changed: "God might have put his magic on it and said 'Don't burn the bushes.'" Here is a semimagical approach. Around the age of eleven, children began to grasp the possibility of symbol or inner experience. "The flames would probably be God; flames that didn't burn," or "God was in it and he was holy, so it couldn't burn." Goldman sums up the responses by saying that the young child explains the phenomenon anthropologically: God intervenes in a human manner. This is followed by semiphysical explanations, with God showing spiritual power. In the third stage the child begins to grasp the idea of symbol.[2]

Another story told to the children was that of the temptation of Jesus in the wilderness.[3] The question asked was whether Jesus could have turned the stone into bread if he had wanted to; and why, if he was hungry, he did not do this. One six-year-old replied, "He didn't know the stone was magic and it could turn into bread." Others were misled by the phrase "by bread *alone*," asserting that he was supposed to eat something with it, like butter or jam. One said "He didn't want to; he wasn't hungry." The eight- to ten-year-olds looked to the authority of God for solving the problem: "God wanted him to stay out in the wilderness for forty days and not eat," or "If he did, he'd be doing what the devil told him. The devil's horrible!" Insight into the spiritual dimensions of

the story is indicated by the age of twelve. "It was a case of
good against evil". Or, "He didn't want to use his power on
things like that. It was too trivial." Goldman concluded that,
up to the age of eight years, the answers were inadequate
and irrelevant. During the next few years, misconceptions
are apparent: Jesus has divine power, so there was no real
test. Eventually, at about the age of twelve, children evidence insight into the dimension of struggle. Only after the
age of fourteen are they able to see the temptation as related
to Jesus' vocation.[4]

Goldman also used pictures in order to find children's responses to the Bible. One was a picture of a child looking at
a lectern Bible of which an open page was torn and scribbled
on.[5] The children were asked how they felt about this. A few
said that no book should be so treated. Many thought it was
especially bad to mutilate a Bible. "Why?" they were asked.
They answered that it was holy, special, and different; it tells
about people who are holy, like God and Jesus. This is circular
reasoning. Asked what makes the Bible different, the children replied, "It's a big book and it's got small print." (Evi-
dently no one had given them a contemporary, large-print
paperbound edition!) Some thought that *holy* meant that it
had holes in it. One child thought, "It's read on Sunday and
Sunday is holy so they call it Holy Bible." Some children held
such views until the age of ten.

In the next stage of cognitive development, the children
who were questioned spoke of the truth of the Bible.[6] While
agreeing that a cookbook is also true, one child saw the special quality of the Bible in that it is a book about God. Asked,
"Are there other books about God?" the child replied, "Yes,
but the Bible's thicker." They also knew that it is special
because it tells about Jesus. At the age of twelve children
were beginning to see more kinds of meaning in the Bible.
"It's a special thing you worship God with and read about

people who've done good. It tells you what to do and what not to do." "It's God's message to his people." Again the stages of development are clear: concrete thought gradually gives way to conceptual thinking.

On the basis of this research, Goldman named three categories for cognitive religious development that parallel Piaget's three categories. Early childhood, ages five to seven, represents prereligious thought. Middle childhood, ages seven to nine, is a period of subreligious thought, becoming more advanced for the nine- to eleven-year-olds. Personal religious thought develops during preadolescence, ages eleven to thirteen, but real conceptual thinking about religious matters cannot be expected until adolescence.

Goldman's Dimensions of Learning

A few years after Goldman's work was completed, a number of religious educators were asked to comment on it.[7] Aware that this was careful research, yielding useful information, some still pointed out that it measured only one dimension of learning. Children understood the stories in their own way.[8] They should not be expected to understand in an adult way nor to have to wait to hear Bible stories until they could comprehend adult meanings. Goldman's reply was that many children who incorrectly interpreted the Bible remember the experience in adolescence and leave the church at a time when they might, if given the information then, be able to understand more clearly what the Bible is saying. Instead, the Bible seems absurd, and people who teach in churches seem untrustworthy. If children were taught only material that could hold meaning for them, much of the Bible could be fresh for adolescents and they could understand the message more fully.

This viewpoint needs serious consideration. Remembering what Piaget said about the way in which very young children interpret strange events as magic, one can see how parallel this is to the way children in the Goldman study interpreted certain biblical events. If miracle equals magic in the comprehension of children, something is wrong. Maybe the time was not right for telling the story.

The Bible is the basic story of the people of God. It has been retold wherever people gather. The authority of the teller and the way in which the story is told are both important, perhaps more so than the Goldman study would suggest. Telling the story to an individual child in a clinical setting, as Goldman did, gives a matter-of-fact aspect that ignores context. When the story is told within a family or church setting by parents or teachers, a sense of wonder is conveyed and the magical element becomes less consequential even if it remains in the child's mind. This does not mean deliberately choosing such stories for use with children, but only that hearing them in the family or at church brings other factors into focus. There is so much material in the Bible that no one should be in a hurry to introduce all of it to very young children.

The Goldman study can alert parents and teachers to the way children interpret material. Their written answers do not tell the full meaning. Children can learn answers sooner than they can express the meaning of those answers. Goldman was able to make his study because children in the English schools had a content-centered biblical curriculum. He chose three highly symbolic stories in order to obtain a wide spread of interpretation. It was unlikely that this particular material would be used with six-year-olds, but it challenged him to discover what materials a six-year-old can understand.

For some, religious education is understood as search more

than the imparting of knowledge; an avenue through which children learn to identify their own questions and needs, articulate these, and seek, in company with others in the class, to find answers.[9] The emphasis is on an understanding of relationship to God that will strengthen the life of each person. Biblical people had this relationship, but their lives may seem unreal and distant to today's children. The teacher can suggest parallels: "Jacob was away from home and lonely when night came, but knowing that God was near made him feel secure." But the children are younger than Jacob, are not being sent away under questionable circumstances, and do not have visions of ladders to heaven. The Jacob story as heritage is a good one, but the children may not identify with it. To understand that God is always near requires stories from the lives of children that evoke remembrances of times when the children may have felt alone. The reassurance comes through the teacher's words and a biblical affirmation such as "I will be with you. I will not fail you or forsake you" (Josh. 1:5).

Religious education is a search in many directions: to understand the meaning of Christian life and commitment, to know what it is to be a member of the Christian community, to realize redemption personally, to know what it means to speak of a world redeemed, to find an identification with Jesus as Lord, and to walk in the way of the cross. Not all of these goals are tasks for the religious education of children. Although the Bible is a primary source through which adults find meaning in the quest, most children are not ready to find identification with biblical events this way.

Relating to Biblical Materials

Goldman states that the goal of his work was to ascertain cognitive learning.[10] This may be one of the less important aspects of biblical study with children. Response to the word God speaks through scripture is primary, and this is affective learning, in which the Bible speaks personally to the learner. There are verses from the Psalms that lift the spirit. Other verses carry reassurance. There are stories with which the child can identify, such as that of Jesus and the children (Mark 10:13, 14). (But there is no need to include the closing sentence [verse 15], which was addressed to adults.)

Symbols have power. Their importance can be observed in the retelling of the Passover story at the Seder celebrations in the Jewish home. The young child may not understand much of the cognitive meaning, and have no sense of historical time, but the tradition is evoked; and with each succeeding year the meaning becomes enriched. So it is for the Christian child learning the narrative of the Last Supper. The theological meaning may not be apparent, but other meanings can be understood: the joy of the disciples feasting with their master, the sense of foreboding, thanksgiving over gifts of food. It will be much later before the words "This is my body . . ." or "The new covenant . . ." have meaning. The symbol is a long time revealing its depth. Even adults interpret these words in various ways.

The function of symbols is to express desires, feelings, and transformed actions. Such interpretation is affected less by cognitive development than by a child's relationships. For example, how frightening or reassuring the story of Abraham and Isaac is, even for older children, depends on whether the child believes a father could sacrifice a child, or whether a child's experience with his or her father gives assurance that this would be an impossibility. The transformation of other family stories from the Bible also reflects this factor—most dramatically, that of Cain and Abel. Aside from the fact that stories written for the Sunday school curriculum leave much to be desired in the way of literary quality, one would hesitate to use such stories with children without knowing about their own anxieties, lest they make some children uncomfortable. On the other hand, identification with people in these stories might help children talk of how they feel about siblings or how they think their parents feel.

Developmental understandings also suggest clues as to how children think about Jesus. To the youngest children, he can do no wrong, as boy or man. He shares the kind of omnipotence accorded to adults, and, in particular, to parents. From age six on, children can see him as a fully human person, although one whose actions were often unusual. (They can understand his healings of people, but they are not able to understand the significance of his healing work as an expression of the presence of the kingdom.) After the age of ten, their perception of the meaning of his life begins to deepen. Titles the Christian community gives him, such as Messiah, Lord, Savior, or Son of God, would not have much meaning until the child had become adolescent. Stories of Jesus should be selected carefully and adult meanings should not be imposed when interpreting for children. The teacher or parent will want children to see him as those who sought his help did, and be drawn to him because he understood their needs.

Teaching Biblical Stories

All the research and critique we have discussed suggests guidelines for the use of the Bible with children. To begin with, how do we view the Bible? We are sharing with children our own understanding, knowledge, and attitudes. Whether the Bible is viewed as the word of God, a guide for living, a witness to the acts of God, or varied literature of the human search for God—this is what parents and teachers share. The first step in teaching should be a serious effort to explore the Bible's meaning within the context of our life in the church. The church collected the documents and formed them into the book we have. Each denomination of the church has its own perception of scripture as the Word of God. How often we read the Bible and the meaning it has for us as inspiration, teaching, comfort, information, or anything else, is important for our teaching. Our church can help us to deepen our understanding by providing opportunities for Bible study and teachers' meetings where the Bible is studied, and by making available study guides such as biblical dictionaries and commentaries. Remember that the clergy are resource persons to whom all may turn with questions.

One should be faithful to the text when teaching. When a Bible story appears in the teaching material, this should be compared with the text. Is the retelling faithful to the original? Does it convey the same meaning? In adapting the story to a child's understanding, has the story writer distorted the meaning? Sometimes the story of the infant Moses has been interpreted as an example of how a little sister helped, and the feeding of the multitude as an act of kindness; both narratives actually are telling about the power and purposes of God expressed in human actions. Story-telling techniques may be used to fill in background details, and conversation makes a lively narrative. But the conversation must faithfully portray the characters into whose mouths the words are placed.

In choosing biblical material or evaluating what is included in a teaching manual, the teacher needs to ask what kinds of identifications the children will make. The age of the person in the biblical story is not as important a factor as the experience. There might be no identification possible with the child Samuel because his life is so different from that of a contemporary child. But all children have problems with brothers and sisters, just as Joseph and his brothers did. No one can make a hero out of young Joseph with children who are quick to put down the boaster. They also have something in common with the disciples who quarreled about who would be greatest in the kingdom. Competitiveness is part of life, at school or at home.

In speaking of models or examples, it is well to remember that, as the gospel stories are retold, hearers identify with those who first heard and responded. We do not identify with Jesus. He is the one who calls, heals, and tells the good news. This point can be made clear by comparing pictures illustrating the story of Zacchaeus. Sometimes the viewer stands with Jesus and the disciples looking up at Zacchaeus. A more accurate interpretation would place Zacchaeus as the central figure, looking down from the tree at Jesus and the disciples. Here the learner identifies with Zacchaeus. Children can appreciate this situation. They, too, are small and cannot see above adults. How wonderful that Jesus noticed Zacchaeus and promised to come to his house! Children also understand Zacchaeus' hidden guilt. What child has not at some time used money intended for some other purpose? "Salvation" as release from guilt after confession and restitution is good news. Teachers will have no difficulty finding more stories once they become aware of ways in which children identify with characters.

Understanding Symbolic Writing

Parents and teachers need to ask what symbols children understand. When in doubt, it is best to keep away from the symbolic. Explaining the rainbow story (Gen. 9:12–17), the teacher may say, "Whenever you see a rainbow, it can remind you of God's promise to take care of everyone." Or in telling about John the Baptist (Mark 1: 4–8): "When John baptized people he was reminding them that God had washed away their sins." (Christian baptism, however, has the broader dimension of dying and rising with Christ.) The cross reminds us that Jesus loved people so much that he died for them. This may not have much meaning beyond the idea that the cross in some strange way reveals God's love. Adults also find the idea profound beyond their full comprehension.

Parables are symbolic forms that young children cannot translate. Through the parables of the kingdom Jesus tried to help people see that God's rule was hidden but was worth every effort to uncover. Children, however, understand these as stories about a woman who rejoiced over finding a lost coin or a man who sold everything for a valuable jewel. They can picture the farmer sowing seeds with varying results, but the application of "sowing the word" is not their way of concrete reasoning. However, the story of the son who left home but was forgiven and restored (and the elder brother who resented this) will remind them of the forgiving love of God. Children cannot be expected to think of themselves as sheep in the parable of the lost sheep, even if they come from places where sheep raising is an industry. No matter how that parable is transformed to show a lost dog or a lost child, young hearers do not put themselves in this place. People who live in industrialized cultures have to make a deliberate effort to identify with the symbol of the sheep. They may do so in reading the Twenty-third Psalm, but the identification doesn't come naturally. Metaphors, similies, parables, symbols, object lessons—all require a cognitive process the young child is not ready to use. In all the pages of the Bible there must be something beyond a few overused stories to evoke the religious response of children.

Teachers and parents need to give serious thought about how to use miracle stories. This is not a matter of one's belief; it is a warning that what adults say might cause children to misunderstand the Bible. When people are healed by the power of God made known through Jesus, children should be able to understand the action as God's work. This is communicated by how the story is written, how it is told, how children perceive it, and how their questions and comments are answered. What the child cannot grasp is better left unexplained until a later time.

If children learn these stories through television, parents and teachers will need to deal with what the children describe, reinterpreting television portrayals of the marvelous into an understanding that these stories aroused a sense of wonder in those who watched, were helped, or wrote down the story. People today echo the astonishment of Jesus' contemporaries, who were "astonished beyond measure" (Mark 7:37). Children need to hear stories of how Jesus entered into the lives of people: visiting, eating, talking, healing, teaching, and comforting. Often he visited a family home for a meal.

Teachers and parents will not avoid the Passion story. This is part of the total experience of the Christian community. Children are aware that this is a significant event. Since they already know the ending of Easter Day, they do not view the crucifixion simply as a cruel and tragic death. With Christians everywhere, they celebrate these events, participating in the drama of redemption. This is the paschal feast, as the oldest hymns remind us. The connection should be emphasized. It is more important than secular symbols of prehistoric fertility rites that have come from the more recent past. The joy of Easter tells the child that Christ is risen and lives among his people.

The Bible was conveyed to the people of Israel for many generations in oral form, as the first remembrances of the words and works of Jesus were later conveyed to the earliest Christian congregations. The forms of writings in the Bible include story, poem, hymns, prayer, and proclamation. There are also literary forms such as The Song of Solomon and the letters of Paul. Story telling is still a basic method for conveying what the Bible has to say. The competent teacher will take time to become an expert story teller. Stories on records and cassettes will provide models.[11] One will soon enjoy putting oneself into the retelling of a story, using voice, hands, and the whole body to make it vivid, and finding satisfaction in the response of the hearers.

Children who hear Bible stories at home bring an enriched experience to their religious education classes. The stories can be told in class without insisting that they must be linked with a lesson or have some application to child experience. Stories can be told or read to early comers. If there is time for juice and crackers, the children will enjoy listening while they eat. When interest centers are used, a small rug and a collection of story books will invite the children to join a story-telling teacher or helper. Whole units may be built around Bible stories, without the need to find a life parallel or point a moral.

Finally, it is helpful to get acquainted with the riches for teaching to be found in biblical affirmations. Teachers fix their attention so fully on using Bible *stories* that they may fail to see what else there is. If the point is to have the Bible speak to the learner, the material may lie elsewhere. The following passages, for example, are helpful: "O give thanks to the Lord, for he is good; for his steadfast love endures for ever" (Ps. 136:1); "When I am afraid, I will put my trust in thee" (Ps. 56:3); "We love, because he first loved us" (John 4:19); "Love one another as I have loved you" (John 15:12); "You are my friends if you do what I command you" (John 15:14).

The Bible is filled with words of trust and assurance. What God has done, he continues to do. The love of God is affirmed by his creative work and his continuing care. Here is where the Bible speaks to the life situation. These words are for everyone, everywhere. A teacher will have no trouble finding words for kindergarten children, or passages and whole psalms for elementary boys and girls. If we do our own searching, we shall find. This is the word of life.

Research in child development has provided an important resource for those concerned about the religious development of children. Within the environment of home and church (as well as school), these children are growing emotionally as well as physically. They are learning how to think and feel. The application of technical developmental theories to religious development can help parents and other teachers guide the moral growth of children, and can give them clues in the sensitive area of nurturing children for Christian commitment. The Bible will speak to children when adults who use the Bible are aware of the "teachable moment" for using selected stories and passages. An awareness of God comes into the life of each child in accordance with an inner timing, and the privilege given parents and teachers is to nurture faith toward that time. This hope can be both an encouragement and a source of joy.

Notes

Preface

1. Shirley Heckman and Iris E. Ferren, *Creating the Congregation's Educational Program,* Elgin, Ill.: Brethren Press, 1976; Joreen Jarrell, ed., *Developing the Congregation's Educational Program,* Philadelphia: Geneva Press, 1976; and St. Louis: Christian Board of Publications, *Planning for Education in the Congregation,* 1974.

Chapter 1: The Child Grows

1. Robert J. Havighurst, *Human Development and Education,* 3rd ed., New York: David McKay, 1962.
2. Erik H. Erikson, "Growth and Crises of the Healthy Personality," *Identity and the Life Cycle: Selected Papers (Psychological Issues,* vol. 1, no. 1, 1959), New York: International Universities Press, pp. 55f.
3. *Ibid.,* pp. 64f.
4. Andre Godin, "Parental Images and the Divine Paternity," *Lumen Vitae,* vol. 19, 1964, pp. 253f.

5. Erikson, *Identity and the Life Cycle: Selected Papers*, p. 82.
6. *Ibid.*, p. 88.

Chapter 2: The Child Thinks

1. Jean Piaget, *Six Psychological Studies*, New York: Random House, 1968, Part I, "The Mental Development of the Child," p. 9.
2. See also J.H. Flavell, *The Developmental Psychology of Jean Piaget*, New York: Van Nostrand, 1963; Mary Ann Spencer Pulaski, *Understanding Piaget*, New York: Harper & Row, 1971; and other interpreters.
3. Jean Piaget, *The Child's Conception of Time*, London: Routledge and Kegan Paul, 1969, p. 259.
4. Jean Piaget, *The Child's Conception of the World*, Totowa, N.J.: Littlefield, Adams and Company, 1975.
5. Jean Piaget, *Play, Dreams and Imitation in Childhood*, New York: Norton, 1962.
6. Jean Piaget, *The Origin of the Idea of Chance in Children*, New York: Norton, 1975, p. 221.
7. Jean Piaget, *The Language and Thought of the Child*, New York: New American Library, 1955; especially pp. 175–202.
8. Jean Piaget, *The Moral Judgment of the Child*, Glencoe, Ill.: The Free Press, 1965.

Chapter 3: The Child Feels

1. One of the more complete outlines of emotional development in children may be found in Elizabeth B. Hurlock, *Child Development*, 4th ed., New York: McGraw-Hill, 1964, pp. 260–324.
2. Richard M. Jones, *Fantasy and Feeling in Education*, New York: Harper & Row, 1970, ch. 3, pp. 276f, ch. 5, pp. 286f.
3. Recent books about the child's understanding of death include: Sylvia Anthony, *The Discovery of Death in Childhood and After*, Boston: Beacon Press, 1972; Marie Fargues, *The Child and the Mystery of Death*, New York: Paulist Press, 1966; Earl L. Grollman, *Talking about Death: A Dialogue Between Parent and Child*, Boston: Beacon Press, 1972; Edgar N. Jackson, *Telling a Child about Death*, New York: Hawthorn, 1975. Elizabeth L. Reed, *Helping Children with the Mystery of Death*, Nashville: Abingdon Press, 1970; Linda J. Vogel, *Helping a Child Understand Death*, Philadelphia: Fortress Press, 1965; Anna W. Wolf, *Helping Your Child Understand Death*, Washington, D.C.: Child Study Association, 1972.
4. Little on the child's own experience of death has been written for general use, most listed studies being technically oriented for professionals on the "management" of death. However, this need has been met by

Myra Bluebond-Langner, *The Private Worlds of Dying Children,* Princeton, N.J.: Princeton University Press, 1978.

Chapter 4: Aspects of Learning

1. B.F. Skinner, *The Technology of Teaching,* New York: Appleton-Century-Crofts, 1968; especially ch. 4, "The Technique of Teaching"; ch. 6, "Teaching Thinking"; ch. 7, "Motivation of the Student"; and ch. 8, "The Creative Student."

Chapter 5: Religious Development

1. David Elkind, "The Child's Concept of Prayer," *Lumen Vitae,* vol. 22, 1967, pp. 441f.
2. The religious understandings of young children have been explored also by Violet Madge in *Children in Search of Meaning,* New York: Morehouse-Barlow Company, 1966, and *Introducing Young Children to Jesus,* New York: Morehouse-Barlow Company, 1971; and Johanna Klink in *Your Child and Religion,* Richmond, Va.: John Knox Press, 1972, and *Teaching Children To Pray,* Philadelphia: Westminster Press, 1975.
3. David Elkind, "The Child's Consciousness of His Religious Identity," *Lumen Vitae,* vol. 19, 1964, pp. 635ff.
4. *Ibid.,* p. 646.
5. P.J. Lawrence, "Children's Thinking about Religion: A Study in Concrete Operational Thinking," *Religious Education,* vol. 60, 1965, pp. 111f.
6. This aspect of the child's understanding of God has been reported by Robert Williams in "A Theory of God-Concept Readiness: From the Piagetian Theories of Child Artificialism and the Origin of Religious Feeling in Children," *Religious Education,* vol. 66, 1971, pp. 631f.

   Other studies on the child's religious development are: Randolph Crump Miller, *Your Child's Religion,* New York: Hawthorn, 1975; R.S. Lee, *Your Growing Child and Religion,* New York: Macmillan, 1963; Marc Oraison, *Love or Constraint?: Some Psychological Aspects of Religious Education,* New York: Paulist Press, 1961. An excellent film on religious development has been done by David Elkind for Geneva Press, entitled *What Do You Think?* This application of Piaget's theories is available from several rental sources.

Chapter 6: Growing into Moral Persons

1. Robert Hogan and Wayne Bahannon, "Ambiguities in the Research Basis of the Cognitive Developmental Base to Moral Education," in

Thomas C. Hennessy, *Values and Moral Development,* New York: Paulist Press, 1976, p. 119.

2. Robert F. Peck and Robert J. Havighurst, *The Psychology of Character Development,* New York: Wiley, 1960; also quoted by Havighurst in an article in Hennessy, *Values and Moral Development,* p. 168.

3. Barry I. Chasan and Jonas F. Soltis, eds., *Moral Education,* New York: Teachers College Press, 1974. Excellent essays from the philosophical viewpoint by ethicists such as William K. Frankena, R.M. Hare, and John Wilson, as well as one by Lawrence Kohlberg on "The Child as Moral Philosopher," pp.131f.

4. The factor of empathy is discussed in a book by Ronald Duska and Mariellen Whalan, *Moral Development: A Guide to Piaget and Kohlberg,* New York: Paulist Press, 1976, especially ch. 2, pp. 80f. They also include practical applications of Kohlberg's stages to religious education. Further methods for teaching will be found in Robert T. Hall and John U. David, *Moral Education in Theory and Practice,* Buffalo: Prometheus Books, 1975, ch. 10, pp. 100f.

5. Sidney B. Simon, *Meeting Yourself Halfway,* Niles, Ill.: Argus Communications, 1974, is a book on value clarification strategies, as is Simon, *Values Clarification: A Handbook of Practical Strategies for Teachers and Students,* New York: Hart Publishing Co., 1972.

6. Helpful material will be found on the Christian perspective in Duska and Whalan, *Moral Development,* pp. 80f. Donald G. Miller, in *The Wing-Footed Wanderer: Conscience and Transcendence,* Nashville: Abingdon Press, 1977, outlines current moral theories and assesses them in the light of the biblical understanding of the transcendence of God.

Chapter 7: A Child's Commitment

1. Philip Greven, *The Protestant Temperament: Patterns of Child-Rearing, Religious Experience, and the Self in Early America,* New York: Knopf, 1977; see Part Two, "Authoritarian Families," "Modes of Evangelical Child-rearing," pp. 21ff.

2. Paul Sangster, *Pity My Simplicity,* London: Epworth Press, 1963, discusses the religious education of children in Wesley's time.

3. Horace Bushnell, *Christian Nurture,* New Haven, Conn: Yale University Press, 1967.

4. Philip Greven, *The Protestant Temperament,* Part Three: "Authoritarian Families," "Moderate Modes of Child-rearing," pp. 151ff.

5. Pierre Babin, *Crisis of Faith: The Religious Psychology of Adolescence,* New York: Herder and Herder, 1964, ch. 2, "The Conversion of Youth," pp. 56f; *Faith and the Adolescent,* New York: Herder and Herder, 1965, ch. 4, "The Religious Possibilities of Adolescents," pp.111 ff.

6. James Fowler, "Toward a Developmental Perspective on Faith," *Religious Education,* vol. 69, pp. 205f.

7. See Gideon C. Yoder, *The Nurture and Evangelism of Children,* Scottdale, Penn.: Herald Press, 1959, p. 158, on the social pressure leading the child attending a membership class to be baptized and become a member of the church.

8. Lewis Joseph Sherrill, *The Struggle of the Soul,* New York: Macmillan, 1951; especially ch. 1, pp. 11 ff.

9. Edward L. Hayes, "Evangelism of Children," in Roy B. Zuck and Robert E. Clark, eds., *Childhood Education in the Church,* Chicago: Moody Press, 1975.

Chapter 8: Religious Development and the Family

1. Specific information on resources may be found in Herbert Arthur Otto, *Marriage and Family Enrichment,* Nashville: Abingdon Press, 1976.

2. Suggestions for family evenings are provided in the periodical *Marriage* (St. Meinrad, Ind.: Abbey Press).

3. See Iris V. Cully and Kendig Brubaker Cully, *An Introductory Theological Wordbook,* Philadelphia: Westminster Press, 1963, for brief discussions of many words in the Christian vocabulary.

4. The most complete and varied program available for such study is to be found in the multimedia program available from Paulist Press, New York.

Chapter 9: The Child in the Christian Community

1. Suggested children's sermons: S. Lawrence Johnson, *The Mouse's Tale and Other Children's Sermons,* Nashville: Abingdon Press, 1978; Jerry Marshall Jordan, *The Brown Bag: A Bag Full of Sermons for Children,* Philadelphia: Pilgrim Press, 1978.

2. David Elkind, "The Child's Consciousness of Religious Identity," *Lumen Vitae,* vol. 19, pp. 635 ff.

3. See Bernadette Kenny, *Children's Liturgies,* New York: Paulist Press, 1977; John Behnke, *A Children's Lectionary* (Cycle A), New York: Paulist Press, 1974; Jack Noble White, *Everything You Need for Children's Worship (Except Children),* Cincinnati: St. Anthony Messenger Press, 1978; David B. Gamm, *Child's Play,* Notre Dame, Ind.: Ave Maria Press, 1978 (fifteen scripture passages highlighting the liturgical seasons arranged for dramatic presentation, grades 3–8).

Chapter 10: Ways of Teaching

1. Jerome S. Bruner, *Toward a Theory of Instruction,* Cambridge, Mass.: Harvard University Press, 1966; especially ch. 6, "The Will to Learn," pp. 113 ff.

2. I first outlined these steps in *The Dynamics of Christian Education,* Philadelphia: Westminster Press, 1958.

Chapter 11: The Bible Speaks to Children

1. Ronald Goldman, *Religious Thinking from Childhood to Adolescence,* New York: Seabury Press, 1969, pp. 104–107.
2. *Ibid,* p. 107.
3. *Ibid.,* pp. 166–170.
4. *Ibid.,* pp. 169–171.
5. *Ibid.,* pp. 69–72.
6. Ronald Goldman, *Readiness for Religion,* London: Routledge and Kegan Paul, 1965, pp. 75–80.
7. *Religious Education,* vol. 63, 1968, pp. 419f.
8. *Ibid.,* pp. 453f.
9. *Ibid.,* p. 443.
10. Goldman, *Religious Thinking from Childhood to Adolescence,* p. 2.
11. John Harrell and Mary Harrell, *To Tell of Gideon: The Art of Storytelling in the Church,* published by the authors, Box 9006, Berkeley, California, is a book with accompanying record and cassette.

Index

Abelard, 97
accommodation, 20
activity, 51 ff.
adaptation, 20
Advent, 64, 111
affection, 34 ff.
affective learning, 32–33
alienation, 66
Anabaptists, 89–90
anger, 36 ff., 66, 108
animals, 35
Anselm, 97
anxiety, 36 ff.
assimilation, 20 ff.
atonement, 97
attitudes, 113 ff.
Augustine, xi, 96, 99
autonomous level, 81–82
autonomy, 5 ff., 81–82

Babin, Pierre, 94
baptism, 89 ff., 101, 109
Beatitudes, 53
bedtime prayer, 106–7
behavior, 42–43, 51 ff., 83 ff.
Bible, xii, 24 ff., 41–42, 43, 45 ff.,
    54, 66, 86–87, 98, 135, 143 ff.
biblical spectaculars, 107
blind children, 59
books, 107, 130
born again, 90 ff., 96 ff.
Bruner, Jerome, xi, 150 ff.
Bushnell, Horace, 90–91

Calvin, John, 89
camping, 111
Cana conference, 109
chance, 26–27
character development, 83–84

character types, 83–84
causal explanation, 28
child evangelism, 97, 102–3
Children in the Church, xiii
Christian Education: Shared Approaches, xiii
Christian Nurture, 90
Christmas, 65 ff., 107, 111, 126, 130
church, 65 ff., 97, 109 ff., 116 ff.
classroom behavior, 51 ff.
cognitive learning, 21, 101–2, 143 ff.
collective monologues, 27
commitment, 93–94, 100
communication, 139–40
competency, 130
concrete-operational stage, 19 ff.
conditioning, xii, 49–50, 77 ff.
conduct, 42–43
confirmation, 93–94, 102
Confraternity of Christian Doctrine, xii
conscience, 10
conventional level, 81
conversation, 38, 140
conversion, 96 ff.
creativity, 53
creeds, xiii, 71–72, 93–94
cross, 25, 97
curiosity, 129

dance, 45
deaf children, 59–60
death, 46 ff.
dedication, 109
development, 63 ff., 78 ff.
developmental categories, 167 ff.
developmental tasks, 3–4
divorce, 105
doubt, 6 ff.
drama, 25, 93, 131
dreams, 23 ff.

Easter, 47, 69, 106, 108, 120, 126, 131, 154
Eastern Orthodox, 92
ecumenism, 127
elementary age, 12 ff., 34–35, 67 ff., 121–22
Elkind, David, 20, 69–70, 122–23
emotionally disturbed children, 60–61
emotions, 41
empathy, 83–84
Erikson, Erik H., xi–xii, 2 ff., 67, 78–79, 94, 130–31
ethical questions, 70
eucharist, 91–92, 101–2, 112
evangelism, 97 ff., 139

faith, 2 ff., 72 ff., 91 ff.
faithing, 94–95
family, 91 ff., 104 ff.
family cluster, 110
family rituals, 67
fear, 39 ff., 136
feelings, 34 ff.
films, 84
flexibility, 8, 131 ff.
forgiveness, 66, 90
formal-operational stage, 20 ff.
Fowler, 94 ff.
Freud, Sigmund, 78 ff.

games, 24 ff., 29–30, 79, 84
Godin, André, xii, 11
Golden Rule, 42, 76, 82, 86
Goldman, Ronald, xi, 20, 67, 69, 81, 143 ff.
Good Friday, 126
grace, 7, 31, 97
grandparents, 6, 110
Greven, Philip, 91
growth, 1 ff., 75 ff.
guilt, 9 ff.

habits, 49, 133
Havighurst, Robert H., 2, 83–84
Heinz dilemma, 76
Holy spirit, 71, 98
homeostasis, 15–16
hostility, 36 ff., 66
Hugo, Victor, 76

identification, 132 ff.
identity, 12
imagination, 53
imitation, 24 ff., 64
individuating/reflexive stage, 95
industry, 12 ff.
infants, 3 ff., 94
inferiority, 12 ff.
initiative, 9 ff.
insight, 83
intergenerational education, 110
International Child Evangelism
  Association, 97
intrusive mode, 9
Irenaeus, 97

Jesus Christ, 24, 26, 29, 66 ff., 96,
  98, 112, 135, 144 ff.
John the Baptist, 152–53
Jones, Richard M., xiii, 44 ff.
Judaism, 102, 106, 111
judgment, 83–84
justice, 29 ff., 72

kindergarten, 9 ff., 155
Kohlberg, Lawrence, 29 ff., 86, 90,
  94 ff.

language, 27
law, 7, 31–32
learning, 13, 24 ff., 48 ff., 128 ff.
learning centers, 61, 140 ff.
learning environment, 56 ff.
lectionary, 117–18
liturgy, 54, 63–64, 69, 106 ff.,
  117 ff.

Lord's Prayer, 11–12, 50, 131
Lord's Supper, 91–92, 101 ff., 120
Lumen Vitae Institute, xii
Luther, Martin, 5, 89
lying, 34–35

magic, 24, 70, 144, 147
Methodists, 90
miracle, 27, 153–54
modeling, 78
morality, 76 ff.
morality of cooperation, 31
moral judgment, 29 ff., 83 ff.
moral realism, 31
moral reasoning, 78, 83 ff.
Mormons, 111
music, 93, 120
mythic-literal stage, 95

observation, 83
Oraison, Marc, xii
Origen, xi

parables, 31, 153
parents, xiii, 64 ff., 104 ff.
parish, 58, 110–11
participation, 137
passion story, 154
pastors, xiii, 57–58, 125 ff.
Paul, 38, 88, 96, 103, 154
Pavlov, 49
Peck, Robert F., 83–84
Pentecost, 120
Piaget, Jean, xi–xii, 17 ff., 27, 67,
  79 ff., 94, 118, 146–47
play, 8, 12–13, 24 ff., 29–30, 84
polar-dialectic stage, 95
postconventional level, 81–82
prayer, 38, 63 ff., 68, 106 ff.,
  119–20, 121–22
preadolescents, 84 ff.
preconventional morality, 80–81
preoperational stage, 18 ff.
Presbyterians, 92

programmed learning, 55
Psalms, 53, 126, 149
psychoanalytic background, xii,
    2–3, 78 ff.
punishment, 40 ff.
puppets, 25, 107
Puritans, 90

Raths, Louis, 85
reasoning, 84–85
reciprocity, 133 ff.
recordings, 107, 155
reinforcement, 51 ff.
relationships, 38 ff., 72 ff., 93–94,
    107 ff.
religious development, 62 ff.
Religious Education Association, xi
religious insights, 38–39
response, 138
resurrection, 47, 69, 106 ff., 120 ff.,
    131, 154
retarded children, 61–62
rewards, 25, 54 ff.
rhythm, 45
role-playing, 25
Roman Catholics, 91, 99, 109,
    126–27
rules, 75 ff.

Santa Claus, 65, 106
schools, community, 59–60, 162–63
seder, 111
sensorimotor stage, 17 ff., 66
sermons, 118–19
shame, 6 ff.
Sherrill, Lewis J., 99
Simon, Sidney, 85
simulation games, 84, 98
sin, 90–91, 97–98
single parents, 109

Skinner, B.F., xi–xii, 50 ff., 134
social contract, 82–83, 86
stages, 3 ff., 80 ff., 91 ff.
story, 36–37, 45–46, 67, 71 ff., 83,
    84, 107, 137, 144 ff., 156
The Struggle of the Soul, 98
"Studies in Deceit," 77
Sunday School, xii, 37 ff., 52 ff.
symbolism, 25–26, 149 ff.
synthetic/conventional stage, 95

table blessings, 106
teachers, 37 ff., 44 ff., 76 ff., 105
teaching methods, 128 ff.
television, 107, 179–80
Ten Commandments, 53, 76
thanksgiving, 68, 106–7
thinking, 16 ff., 20 ff., 27 ff., 130 ff.
Thompson, Francis, 96
time, 22 ff.
toddlers, 6 ff.
trinity, 71–72
trust, 2 ff., 155–56
truth, 70–71

universal ethical principle, 82–83
universalizing stage, 82–83, 95–96

values, 10, 32, 75 ff., 84 ff.
values clarification, 84 ff.

Watson, John, 50
Wesley, John, 96, 100
why questions, 28 ff.
worship, 117 ff.
writing, 131
wrong-doing, 66, 119

Yoder, Gideon C., 98